Street by Street

EASTBOURNE
HAILSHAM

Beachy Head, East Dean, Hampden Park, Langney, Pevensey Bay, Polegate, Westham, Willingdon

1st edition August 2002

© Automobile Association Developments Limited 2002

Ordnance Survey® This product includes map data licensed from Ordnance Survey® with the permission of the Controller of Her Majesty's Stationery Office. © Crown copyright 2002. All rights reserved. Licence No: 399221.

Published by AA Publishing (a trading name of Automobile Association Developments Limited, whose registered office is Millstream, Maidenhead Road, Windsor, Berkshire SL4 5GD. Registered number 1878835).

The Post Office is a registered trademark of Post Office Ltd. in the UK and other countries.

Schools address data provided by Education Direct.

One-way street data provided by:

Tele Atlas © Tele Atlas N.V.

Mapping produced by the Cartographic Department of The Automobile Association. A00965b

A CIP Catalogue record for this book is available from the British Library.

Printed by GRAFIASA S.A., Porto Portugal.

The contents of this atlas are believed to be correct at the time of the latest revision. However, the publishers cannot be held responsible for loss occasioned to any person acting or refraining from action as a result of any material in this atlas, nor for any errors, omissions or changes in such material. This does not affect your statutory rights. The publishers would welcome information to correct any errors or omissions and to keep this atlas up to date. Please write to Publishing, The Automobile Association, Fanum House (FH17), Basing View, Basingstoke, Hampshire, RG21 4EA.

Ref: ML171

G000069187

Key to map symbols	ii
Key to map pages	1
Enlarged scale pages	2-3
Street by Street	4-25
Index – towns & villages	26
Index – streets	27-31
Index – featured places	31-32

Junction 9	Motorway & junction	··················	Airport runway	PH	Public house AA recommended
	Motorway service area	— · — · — · —	County, administrative boundary		Restaurant AA inspected
Services					
	Primary road single/dual carriageway		Mounds		Theatre or performing arts centre
	Primary road service area	93	Page continuation 1:15,000		Cinema
Services					
	A road single/dual carriageway	7	Page continuation to enlarged scale 1:10,000		Golf course
	B road single/dual carriageway		River/canal, lake, pier	▲	Camping AA inspected
	Other road single/dual carriageway		Aqueduct, lock, weir		Caravan site AA inspected
	Minor/private road, access may be restricted	465 ▲ Winter Hill	Peak (with height in metres)		Camping & caravan site AA inspected
← ←	One-way street		Beach		Theme park
	Pedestrian area		Coniferous woodland		Abbey, cathedral or priory
----------	Track or footpath		Broadleaved woodland		Castle
	Road under construction		Mixed woodland		Historic house or building
⌐ - - - ⌐	Road tunnel		Park	Wakehurst Place NT	National Trust property
AA	AA Service Centre		Cemetery	M	Museum or art gallery
P	Parking		Built-up area		Roman antiquity
P+	Park & Ride		Featured building		Ancient site, battlefield or monument
	Bus/coach station		City wall		Industrial interest
	Railway & main railway station	A&E	Hospital with 24-hour A&E department		Garden
	Railway & minor railway station	PO	Post Office		Arboretum
⊖	Underground station		Public library		Farm or animal centre
⊖	Light railway & station	i	Tourist Information Centre		Zoological or wildlife collection
+++++++++	Preserved private railway		Petrol station Major suppliers only		Bird collection
LC	Level crossing	†	Church/chapel		Nature reserve
•—•—•—	Tramway		Public toilets	V	Visitor or heritage centre
- - - - - -	Ferry route		Toilet with disabled facilities		Country park
					Cave
					Windmill
					Distillery, brewery or vineyard

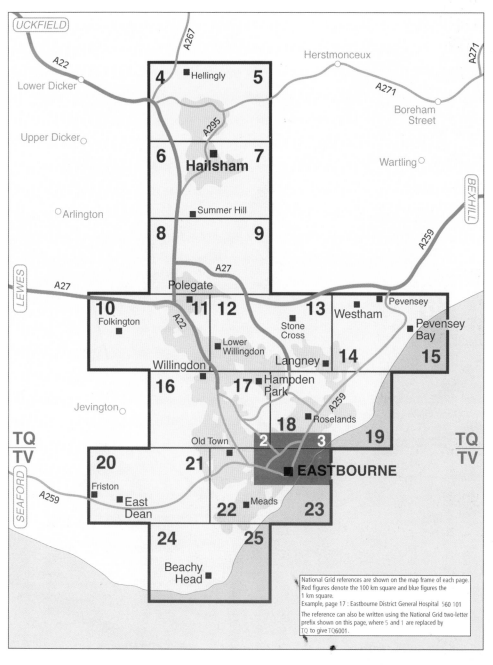

UCKFIELD

A22

A267

Lower Dicker

Herstmonceux

A271

Boreham Street

Upper Dicker

4 Hellingly 5

A295

Wartling

6 Hailsham 7

Arlington

Summer Hill

8 9

BEXHILL

A259

A27

Polegate

A27

LEWES

A27

A22

10 Folkington 11 12 13 Westham Pevensey

Pevensey Bay

Stone Cross

Lower Willingdon

Willingdon Langney 14 15

16 17 Hampden Park

Jevington

A259

18 Roselands

TQ
TV

Old Town 2 3 19

20 Friston 21 EASTBOURNE TQ
TV

SEAFORD

A259

East Dean 22 Meads 23

24 25

Beachy Head

National Grid references are shown on the map frame of each page. Red figures denote the 100 km square and blue figures the 1 km square.
Example, page 17 : Eastbourne District General Hospital 560 101
The reference can also be written using the National Grid two-letter prefix shown on this page, where 5 and 1 are replaced by TQ to give TQ6001.

Enlarged scale pages 1:10,000

.3 inches to 1 mile

miles 1/4

kilometres 1/4 1/2

Scale of main map pages 1:15,000

4.2 inches to 1 mile

0 1/4 miles 1/2

0 1/4 kilometres 3/4

F St Philip's Avenue G **Roselands** H 18 J K

Avenue
Marlow
Recycling Centre
Brydges Cl
churchvale Rd
Willoughby
Archery Youth Centre
A259
St Andrew's CE Infant School
Winchelsea Road
squ
Centre

Fort Fun & Rocky's Adventure Land

Fitzmaurice Avenue
Roselands Avenue
Baillie Av
Rye St
Rye St
Sand
St
Rve St
Wartling
63
1

Woodgate
Windermere Crescent
Roselands Close
Belle Vue Rd
Avenue
PO
Romney st
Winifred Lee Health Centre
Eastbourne United FC
Crumbles Pond
Prince's Park
Royal Parade

Roselands Infant School
Roselands Road

La
Channel
Road
Seaford Road
View
Road
Desmond Road
Guestling Road

Ringwood Road

SEASIDE
BEACH RD
Seabeach
Fairlight Road
Latimer Road
Bexhill Road
Sidley Road
Wannock Road
Penhale Road
Road
2

A2021
Kerrara Ter
Fydneve st
St Josephs RC School
Glennys Estate
Eshton Rd
B2106
Beachy
Royal Parade
P
Lifeboat Station
Butterfly Centre

100
Mona Rd
Kilda Rd
Whitley Rd
Beamsley Rd
Carlton Road
Bardenon Rd
Latimer Road
SIDLEY ROAD
B2106
Royal Parade
P
Fishermen's Club
Eastbourne Sovereign Sailing Club
3

Gilbert Road
Leslie street
Addingham Road
Latimer Road
P
Treasure Island Play Centre

Oxford Rd
Springfield Rd
A259
Redoubt Rd
Hanover Rd
Warrior square
St James Rd
Halton Rd
Rystone Road
PARADE
The Redoubt Fortress and Museum
4

Seaside Medical Centre
Sheen Rd
Cambridge Rd
Latimer Rd
TA Centre
Hotel
Pavilion
Gardens

St Aubyn's Rd
SEASIDE
B2106
Bayham Rd
ROYAL
5

Burfield Rd
Leaf Hall
Hotel

Marine Road
MARINE PDE
B2106
PO
6

099

PIER
7

Eastbourne Pier

F 562 G H J K 63

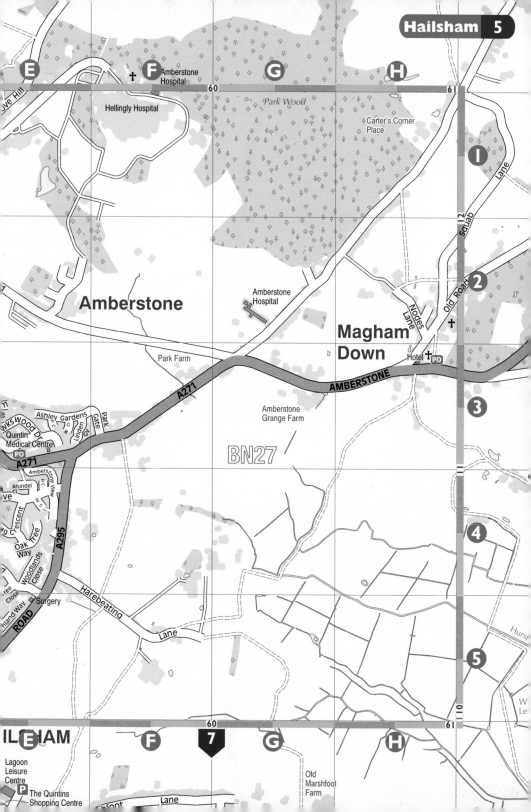

E

✝ F Amberstone Hospital

G

H

Hellingly Hospital

60

61

Park Wood

Carter's Corner Place

I

Squab Lane

Old Road

2

Nodes Lane

Amberstone

Amberstone Hospital

Magham Down

Hotel ✝ PO

✝

Park Farm

Park Gate

A271

AMBERSTONE

3

Ashley Gardens

Linden

WKSWOOD Dr

Quintin Medical Centre

PO

A271

Amberstone View

Amberstone Grange Farm

BN27

Arundel CI

HC

HC

HC

Crescent

Oak Tree Way

A295

4

ve

Woodlands Close

Tree Close

land Way

Surgery

Harebeating

ROAD

Lane

5

Hurst

W Le

60

61

110

IL E HAM

E

F

7

G

H

Lagoon Leisure Centre

P The Quintins Shopping Centre

Old Marshfoot Farm

Lane

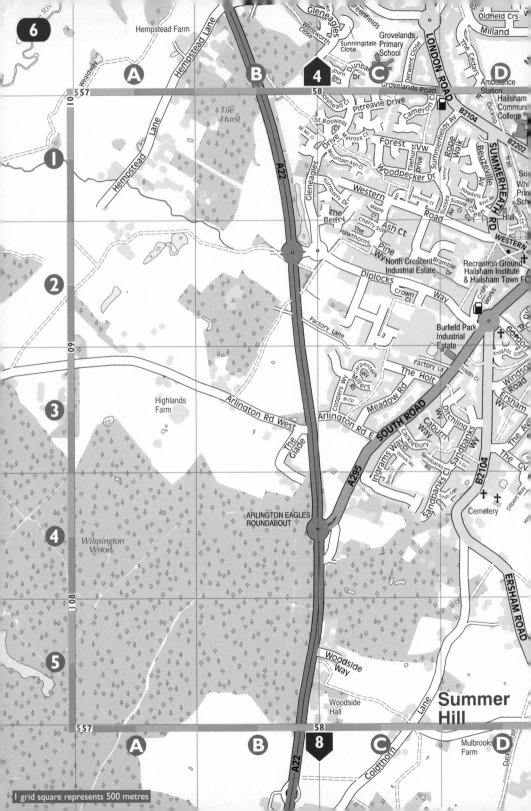

E F 5 G H

60 61

ILSHAM

Lagoon
Leisure
Centre
P
The Quintins
Shopping Centre
Surgery
Vicarage Fields
Shopping Centre
Council
Building
Cattle Market

Marshfoot Lane

Marshlands CP
School

Old
Marshfoot
Farm

St Marys
Av

Greenacres Dr

Greenwich

Newton Ct

Vega Close

Orion Close

The Gages

Kestrel Park

Ct

observatory
Vw

Gemma
Close

St Marys Avenue

Market St

Southdown

The Styles

Bayham Road

Mill Road

observatory
Vw

The Acorns

Bowley Road

The Stringwalk

Archery Walk

anks Rd

Fletcher Close

Peiham
Crs

New Barn
Close

Swan

Howard Ct

Butts Fld

Road

Lion House

Mill Road

ville Rd

Mr Y

Road
ustrial
ate

Swan
Business
Centre

Station Road

Swan Barn
Business Centre

Old Swan Lane

White Dyke
Farm

Station Road

Downash

Slyes
Farm

61

60

09

108

E F 9 G H

I

2

3

4

5

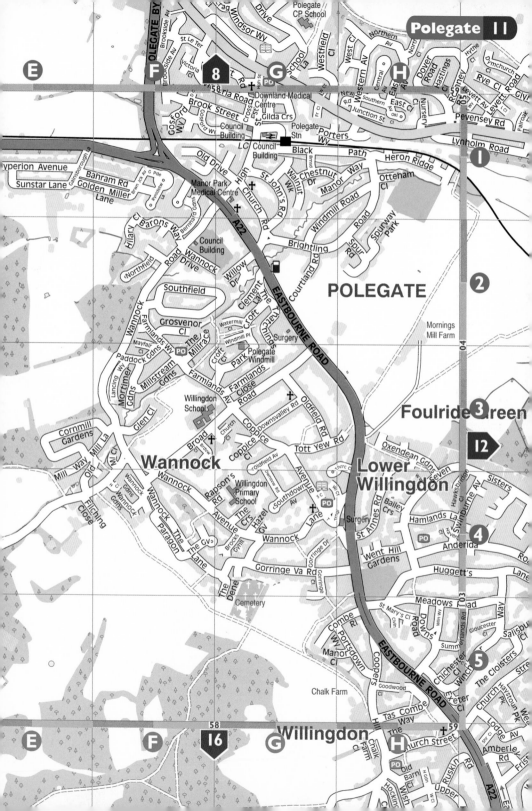

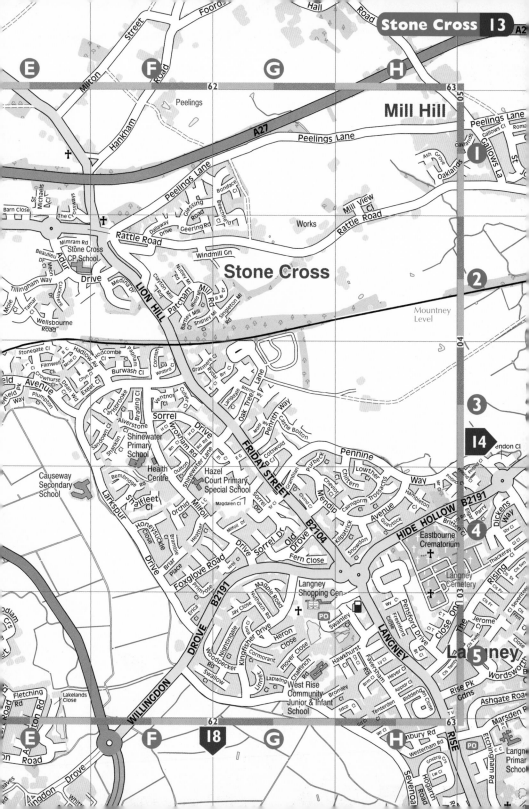

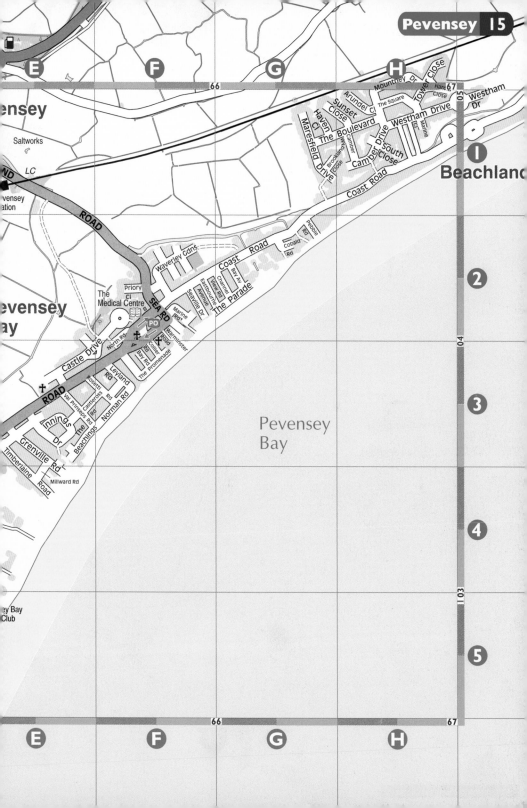

E   F   G   H   67   05   Westham Dr

66

Mountney Dr   Tower Close   Hard Close

Pevensey   Arundel Cl   Sunset Close   The Square

Saltworks   Haven Ct   The Boulevard   Marine   Westham Drive

LC   Maresfield Drive   Brookland Wood Close   Camber Close   Camber Drive   South Close

ND   Pevensey ation   Beachland

Pevensey Bay   Coast Road

Pebble Rd

Cobald Rd

Waverley Gdns   Coast Road

The Priory Cl Medical Centre   Channel View Rd   Bay Av

SEA RD   Marine Rd   Eastbourne Avenue   Seaville Dr   The Parade

PO   Warminster

Castle Drive   North Rd   Collier Rd   The Promenade   Road   Bay Rd

ROAD   Leviland Rd   Rosetti Rd   Norman Rd

Val Princess Rd   Casterross Rd

innings   Dr   The Beachings

Grenville Rd

Timberlaine Road   Millward Rd

Pevensey
Bay

ey Bay
Club

E   F   G   H

66   67

2

04

3

103

4

5

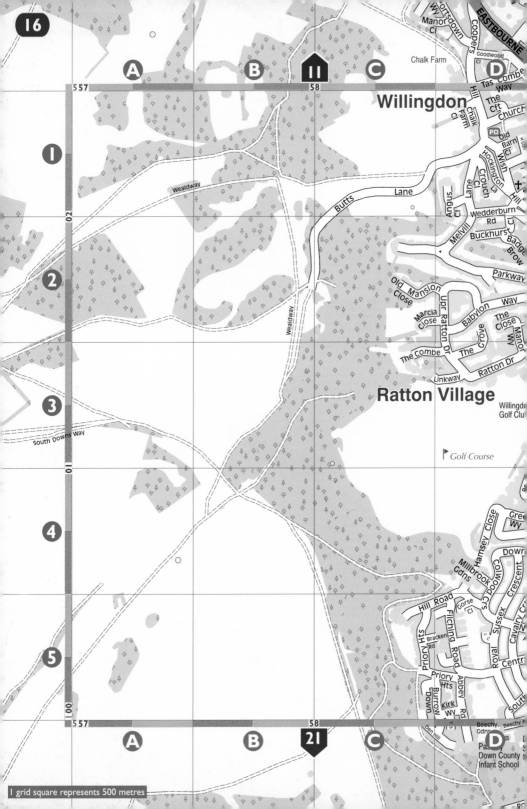

16

A   B   **11**   C   Chalk Farm   D

5 57   58

Willingdon

Chalk Farm Cl

The Cft

Church

PO   Old Barn Cl

Wish

Hockington La

Crouch   Wedderburn Rd

Angus Cl   Buckhurst Cl

Melvill   Badger Brow

1

02

Wealdway   Butts   Lane

Parkway

Old Mansion Close

Marcia Close

Babylon Way   The Close

2

Wealdway

Upr Ratton Dr   The Grove   Manor Wy

The Combe   Ratton Dr

Linkway

3

01

Ratton Village

Willingdon Golf Club

South Downs Way

Golf Course

4

Hamsey Close   Gree Wy

Downs

Millbrook Gdns

Colwood Crs   Crescent

5

00

Hill Road   Gorse Cl   Sussex

Fliching Road   Roya   Cavalry

Priory Hts   Bracken Rd   Centr

Priory Hts   Abbey Rd

Burrow Down   Kirk Wy   South

5 57   58   Beechy   Beechy

A   B   **21**   C   D

Den Hill

Pas

Down County Infant School

1 grid square represents 500 metres

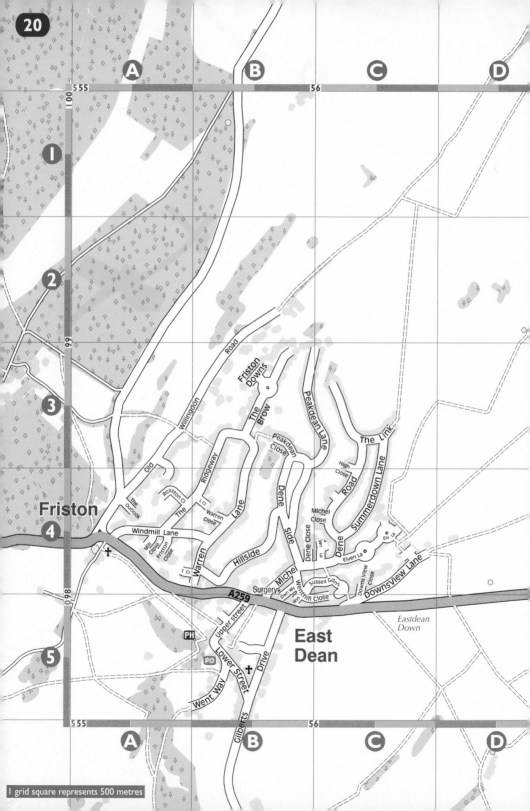

E   F   **16**   G   H

58

59

Priory Hts

Brackeni Rd

Priory Road

Abbey Rd

South Avenue

Victoria Drive

Victoria Crs

Albert Rd

Green

Priory Burrow Down

Kirk Wy

St

Den Hill

Beechy Gdns

Beechy Avenue

South Avenue

Victoria Gdns

Victoria Gdns

PO

Pashley Down County Infant School

Downs Special School

I

Coom Gdn

Nor Road

Chamb Rd

Victoria Road

Peppercombe Road

Osborne Road

Longland Road

Dillingburgh Road

Broomfield

Bodmin Close

Sancroft Road

Manvers Rd

Cherry Gdn Rd

Barcombe Close

Downsi Close

Upwil

2

Wealdway

Upland Rd

Pashley

3

Lindsay Cl

Compton

Foredown Close

ea Down

Ringwood

Golf Course

EAST DEAN ROAD

22

Eastbourne Downs Golf Club

4

South Downs Way

A259

B2103   WARREN

Rochester Close

HILL

B2103

5

Lincol se

Warr

Cranbor

AN ROAD

120

24

A   B   **21**   C   D

5 57   58

Crapham Down

Black Robin Farm

1

97

Long Down

2

Bullock Down

3

96

Beachy H
Countryside
(Visitor Ce

4

Hodcombe Farm

Bea

South   Downs   Way

5

095

Sussex Heritage Coast

Beachy Head Lighthouse

Beachy Hea

5 57   58

A   B   C   D

B2103

I grid square represents 500 metres

Upper Ca...
Upper
Warren Cl
Salisbury Road
Warren Cl
Close
Salisbury
Road
Cra... e Avenue
Lordaine Close
Head
Beachy
Mds Brw
Road
C rd
Road
The Village
Meads
De Walden Ms
Meads Street
Dalton Rd
Milnthorpe Road
Derwent Road
Chesterfield Road
Staveley Road
Buxton Road
Holbrook Close
Chesterfield Gardens
† University
Bolsover Road
EDW...

E   F   22 G   H

60   Darley Road   KING   61
HEAD
UPPER
DUKE'S DR
B2103
Combe
Baslow Road
Road
Rowsley Road
University of Brighton
Edensor Road
Wellcome Crs
St Andrews School
All Saints Hospital
Cliff Road
DUKE'S DR
Holywell Road
St Bedes Preparatory School

I

97

B2103
UPPER   DUKE'S
DRIVE

2

S Downs Way
Holywell

3

96

4

Cow Gap

5

095

60   61
E   F   G   H

Amberstone	5 F2	Hailsham	7 E1	Mill Hill	13 H1
Beachlands	15 H1	Hampden Park	17 G1	Old Town	22 B1
Dittons	12 C1	Hellingly	4 B1	Pevensey	14 D1
Downside	17 E5	Langney	13 H5	Pevensey Bay	15 E2
Eastbourne	2 A4	Lower Horsebridge	4 A2	Polegate	11 G2
East Dean	20 B5	Lower Willingdon	11 H4	Ratton Village	16 D3
Folkington	10 C3	Magham Down	5 H2	Roselands	18 C3
Foulride Green	11 H3	Meads	22 C5	St Anthony's Hill	18 D2

Stone Cross
Summer Hill
Upper Horsebridge
Upperton
Wannock
Westham
Willingdon

USING THE STREET INDEX

Street names are listed alphabetically. Each street name is followed by its postal town or area locality, the Postcode District, the page number, and the reference to the square in which the name is found.

Standard index entries are shown as follows:

Abbey Rd *EDN/EASTW* BN20 ....**16** D5

Street names and selected addresses not shown on the map due to scale restrictions are shown in the index with an asterisk:

Bay Pond Rd *EAST* * BN21 ....**22** B1

GENERAL ABBREVIATIONS

ACC	ACCESS	E	EAST	LDG	LODGE	R	R
ALY	ALLEY	EMB	EMBANKMENT	LGT	LIGHT	RBT	ROUNDAB
AP	APPROACH	EMBY	EMBASSY	LK	LOCK	RD	R
AR	ARCADE	ESP	ESPLANADE	LKS	LAKES	RDG	R
ASS	ASSOCIATION	EST	ESTATE	LNDG	LANDING	REP	REPL
AV	AVENUE	EX	EXCHANGE	LTL	LITTLE	RES	RESER
BCH	BEACH	EXPY	EXPRESSWAY	LWR	LOWER	RFC	RUGBY FOOTBALL
BLDS	BUILDINGS	EXT	EXTENSION	MAG	MAGISTRATE	RI	R
BND	BEND	F/O	FLYOVER	MAN	MANSIONS	RP	R
BNK	BANK	FC	FOOTBALL CLUB	MD	MEAD	RW	R
BR	BRIDGE	FK	FORK	MDW	MEADOWS	S	SC
BRK	BROOK	FLD	FIELD	MEM	MEMORIAL	SCH	SCH
BTM	BOTTOM	FLDS	FIELDS	MKT	MARKET	SE	SOUTH
BUS	BUSINESS	FLS	FALLS	MKTS	MARKETS	SER	SERVICE A
BVD	BOULEVARD	FLS	FLATS	ML	MALL	SH	SH
BY	BYPASS	FM	FARM	ML	MILL	SHOP	SHOP
CATH	CATHEDRAL	FT	FORT	MNR	MANOR	SKWY	SK\
CEM	CEMETERY	FWY	FREEWAY	MS	MEWS	SMT	SUM
CEN	CENTRE	FY	FERRY	MSN	MISSION	SOC	SOC
CFT	CROFT	GA	GATE	MT	MOUNT	SP	S
CH	CHURCH	GAL	GALLERY	MTN	MOUNTAIN	SPR	SP
CHA	CHASE	GDN	GARDEN	MTS	MOUNTAINS	SQ	SQU
CHYD	CHURCHYARD	GDNS	GARDENS	MUS	MUSEUM	ST	STI
CIR	CIRCLE	GLD	GLADE	MWY	MOTORWAY	STN	STA
CIRC	CIRCUS	GLN	GLEN	N	NORTH	STR	STR
CL	CLOSE	GN	GREEN	NE	NORTH EAST	STRD	STR
CLFS	CLIFFS	GND	GROUND	NW	NORTH WEST	SW	SOUTH V
CMP	CAMP	GRA	GRANGE	O/P	OVERPASS	TDG	TRAI
CNR	CORNER	GRG	GARAGE	OFF	OFFICE	TER	TERF
CO	COUNTY	GT	GREAT	ORCH	ORCHARD	THWY	THROUGH
COLL	COLLEGE	GTWY	GATEWAY	OV	OVAL	TNL	TUN
COM	COMMON	GV	GROVE	PAL	PALACE	TOLL	TOLL
COMM	COMMISSION	HGR	HIGHER	PAS	PASSAGE	TPK	TURN
CON	CONVENT	HL	HILL	PAV	PAVILION	TR	TR
COT	COTTAGE	HLS	HILLS	PDE	PARADE	TRL	T
COTS	COTTAGES	HO	HOUSE	PH	PUBLIC HOUSE	TWR	TO\
CP	CAPE	HOL	HOLLOW	PK	PARK	U/P	UNDER
CPS	COPSE	HOSP	HOSPITAL	PKWY	PARKWAY	UNI	UNIVER
CR	CREEK	HRB	HARBOUR	PL	PLACE	UPR	UP
CREM	CREMATORIUM	HTH	HEATH	PLN	PLAIN	V	V
CRS	CRESCENT	HTS	HEIGHTS	PLNS	PLAINS	VA	VA
CSWY	CAUSEWAY	HVN	HAVEN	PLZ	PLAZA	VIAD	VIAD
CT	COURT	HWY	HIGHWAY	POL	POLICE STATION	VIL	V
CTRL	CENTRAL	IMP	IMPERIAL	PR	PRINCE	VIS	V
CTS	COURTS	IN	INLET	PREC	PRECINCT	VLG	VILL
CTYD	COURTYARD	IND EST	INDUSTRIAL ESTATE	PREP	PREPARATORY	VLS	VIL
CUTT	CUTTINGS	INF	INFIRMARY	PRIM	PRIMARY	VW	V
CV	COVE	INFO	INFORMATION	PROM	PROMENADE	W	W
CYN	CANYON	INT	INTERCHANGE	PRS	PRINCESS	WD	W
DEPT	DEPARTMENT	IS	ISLAND	PRT	PORT	WHF	WH
DL	DALE	JCT	JUNCTION	PT	POINT	WK	W
DM	DAM	JTY	JETTY	PTH	PATH	WKS	WA
DR	DRIVE	KG	KING	PZ	PIAZZA	WLS	WI
DRO	DROVE	KNL	KNOLL	QD	QUADRANT	WY	Y
DRY	DRIVEWAY	L	LAKE	QU	QUEEN	YD	Y
DWGS	DWELLINGS	LA	LANE	QY	QUAY	YHA	YOUTH HO\

POSTCODE TOWNS AND AREA ABBREVIATIONS

EAST	Eastbourne	HAIL	Hailsham	LW/ROSE	Lower Willingdon/Roselands
EDN/EASTW	East Dean/Eastbourne west	LGNY	Langney	PEV	Pevensey
				POLE	Pol
				SEAF	Se

A

...y Rd EDN/EASTW BN20 ......16 D5
...dale Rd POLE BN26 ......12 A1
...n Rd LW/ROSE BN22 ......12 B5
...corns HAIL BN27 ......7 F2
...gham Rd LW/ROSE BN22 ...3 G3
...Dr PEV BN24 ......13 E2
...t Rd POLE BN26 ......8 B5
...t Ter EAST BN21 ......17 E5
...n Rd LW/ROSE BN22 ......2 E3
...CI LGNY BN23 ......18 C2
...ndra Rd LW/ROSE BN22 ...18 D4
...gton Rd LW/ROSE BN22 ...19 F2
...ton CI EDN/EASTW BN20 ...22 A3
...stone CI LGNY BN23 ......13 F3
...rley Rd EAST BN21 ......17 E1
...rstone HAIL BN27 ......5 G3
...rstone Vw HAIL BN27 ......5 F4
...orage Wy LGNY BN23 ......14 D5
...rida Rd LW/ROSE BN22 ...11 H4
...sey Av HAIL BN27 ......4 C4
...s CI EDN/EASTW BN20 ...16 D3
...gton Rd LW/ROSE BN22 ...2 A3
...ti CI LGNY BN23 ......19 E3
...Pk HAIL BN27 ......6 C2
...dore CI LGNY BN23 ......13 H5
...ary Wk HAIL BN27 ......7 E3
...ton Rd EAST BN21 ......2 A6
...ton Rd East HAIL BN27 ......6 B3
...ton Rd West HAIL BN27 ......6 B3
...............................4 C4
...ns Dwellings EAST * BN21 ...2 B7
...del CI HAIL BN27 ......5 E4
...BN24 ......15 H1
...Wy PEV BN24 ......12 D2
...ton Rd EDN/EASTW BN20 ...22 C4
...CI EDN/EASTW BN20 ......22 D5
...mpstead PI EAST * BN21 ...2 A7
...rnham Gdns EAST BN21 ...17 G5
...rnham PI HAIL BN27 ......2 C1
...rnham Rd EAST BN21 ......22 C1
...LW/ROSE BN22 ......12 C2
...t HAIL BN27 ......6 C2
...rd CI HAIL BN27 ......7 E2
...rd Rd EAST BN21 ......2 B6
...rd Sq EAST BN21 ......2 B5
...ate Rd LGNY BN23 ......14 A5
...n HAIL BN27 ......13 H1
...gton Rd LW/ROSE BN22 ...18 A1
...y Gdns HAIL BN27 ......5 E3
...n Rd LW/ROSE BN22 ......12 C5
...e Av LW/ROSE BN22 ......2 E1
...stan CI LGNY BN23 ......19 F2
...tic Dr LGNY BN23 ......19 F2
...ton CI EDN/EASTW BN20 ...16 D4
...ue La EAST BN21 ......2 B5
...ue Ms EAST * BN21 ......2 B5
...ue PI EAST * BN21 ......2 B5
...venue EAST BN21 ......2 B5
...............................6 D3
...dale Rd LW/ROSE BN22 ...3 F2
...bury Av LGNY BN23 ......19 E2
...e CI LGNY BN23 ......19 F3

B

...on Wy EDN/EASTW BN20 ...16 D2
...ers Brow
...EASTW BN20 ......16 D2
...esmere Rd LW/ROSE BN22 ...18 E1
...am Rd POLE BN26 ......11 E1
...y Crs LW/ROSE BN22 ......11 H4
...e Av LW/ROSE BN22 ......3 G1
...rs Farm Pk HAIL * BN27 ......4 C2
...'s Rd EAST BN21 ......22 B2
...well Rd EAST BN21 ......17 G2
...win Av EAST BN21 ......17 E4
...ombe CI EDN/EASTW BN20...21 H2
...en Rd LW/ROSE BN22 ......3 G3
...ing CI LGNY BN23 ......13 H5
...CI HAIL BN27 ......5 E5
...BN24 ......13 E1
...ns Wy POLE BN26 ......14 A5
...er Reef Wy LGNY BN23 ......14 C5
...ey Mill CI PEV BN24 ......13 F2
...n Wy EDN/EASTW BN20 ...25 F1
...ford CI LGNY BN23 ......13 H5
...Rd EAST BN21 ......2 B7
...e Crs HAIL BN27 ......7 E1
...e Rd HAIL BN27 ......5 E5
...PEV BN24 ......15 G2

Bayham Rd HAIL BN27 ......7 F2
  LW/ROSE BN22 ......3 G4
Bay Pond Rd LW/ROSE * BN21 ...22 B1
Bay Rd PEV BN24 ......15 F3
Bay Tree La POLE BN26 ......8 B4
The Beachings PEV BN24 ......15 E3
Beach Ms LW/ROSE * BN22 ...3 H2
Beach Rd LW/ROSE BN22 ......3 G2
Beachy Head Rd
  EDN/EASTW BN20 ......22 A5
Beamsley Rd LW/ROSE BN22 ...3 G3
Beatrice La EAST BN21 ......2 A5
Beatty Rd LGNY BN23 ......19 E4
Beaulieu Dr PEV BN24 ......13 E2
Beckenham CI HAIL BN27 ......4 D3
Bedford Gv EAST BN21 ......2 B4
Bedfordwell Rd EAST BN21 ......2 B4
Beechfield CI PEV BN24 ......13 G1
Beechwood HAIL BN27 ......6 D4
Beechwood Crs
  EDN/EASTW BN20 ......22 B2
Beechy Av EDN/EASTW BN20...21 H1
Beechy Gdns EDN/EASTW BN20 ...21 H1
The Belfry HAIL BN27 ......6 C1
Bell Banks Rd HAIL BN27 ......7 E3
Belle Vue Rd LW/ROSE BN22 ...3 G1
Belmore Rd LW/ROSE BN22 ......3 F4
Beltring Rd EAST BN21 ......2 B4
Beltring Ter LW/ROSE BN22 ......3 F4
Bembridge Rd LGNY BN23 ......13 F4
Benbow Av LGNY BN23 ......19 E4
Benjamin CI LW/ROSE BN22 ...12 D5
Beristede CI EDN/EASTW BN20 ...22 C4
Bermuda PI LGNY BN23 ......19 G3
Bernard La EAST BN21 ......2 A5
Bernhard Gdns POLE BN26 ......11 F2
Berwick CI LW/ROSE BN22 ......12 A4
Beuzeville Av HAIL BN27 ......6 D1
Beverington Rd EAST BN21 ......17 F4
Beverington Rd EAST BN21 ......17 F4
Bexhill Rd LW/ROSE BN22 ......3 H2
Bexley CI HAIL BN27 ......4 D4
Biddenden CI LGNY BN23 ......13 H5
Bilbury Ms EAST * BN21 ......2 B3
Binsted CI LW/ROSE BN22 ......12 C5
Birch Rd LGNY BN23 ......18 C3
Birch Wy HAIL BN27 ......6 D3
Birling St EDN/EASTW BN20 ......22 A1
Black Pth POLE BN26 ......11 G1
Blacksmiths Copse HAIL BN27 ......6 C1
Blackthorn Rd LW/ROSE BN22 ...12 C5
Blackwater Rd
  EDN/EASTW BN20 ......22 D4
Blakes Wy LGNY BN23 ......19 F4
Blatchington Mill Dr PEV BN24 ...13 G2
Blenheim Wy POLE BN26 ......12 B1
Bodiam Crs LW/ROSE BN22 ......3 F4
Bodmin CI EDN/EASTW BN20 ...21 H2
Bolsover Rd EDN/EASTW BN20 ...22 C5
Bolton Rd EAST BN21 ......2 C7
Boniface CI PEV BN24 ......13 G1
Borough La EDN/EASTW BN20 ...22 B2
Borrowdale CI LGNY BN23 ......13 G3
Boscawen CI LGNY BN23 ......19 F3
Boship CI LGNY BN23 ......19 F3
Boston CI LGNY BN23 ......19 F3
The Boulevard PEV BN24 ......15 G1
Bourne St LW/ROSE BN22 ......2 E5
Bowley Rd HAIL BN27 ......7 E2
Bowood Av LW/ROSE BN22 ...18 B4
Bracken Rd EDN/EASTW BN20 ...16 C5
Bradford St EAST BN21 ......22 A2
Brading Rd LGNY BN23 ......13 F3
Bramble CI LGNY BN23 ......13 F4
Bramble Dr HAIL BN27 ......6 C2
Bramley Rd POLE BN26 ......12 A1
Brampton Rd LW/ROSE BN22 ...17 H1
Brampton Vls EAST * BN21 ......22 C1
Brand Rd LW/ROSE BN22 ......17 G1
Branston Rd LW/ROSE BN22 ...17 H1
Brassey Av LW/ROSE BN22 ...17 G1
Brassey Pde LW/ROSE * BN22 ...17 H1
Brede CI LW/ROSE BN22 ......18 D4
Brendon CI LGNY BN23 ......14 A3
Briar PI LGNY BN23 ......13 G3
Bridge End PEV BN24 ......14 D1
Bridgemere Rd LW/ROSE BN22 ...18 B4
Brightland Rd
  EDN/EASTW BN20 ......22 B2
Brighting Rd POLE BN26 ......11 G2
Britland Est LW/ROSE * BN22 ...18 C5
Britten CI LGNY BN23 ......13 H4
Broad Oak CI LGNY BN23 ......13 H5
Broad Rd EDN/EASTW BN20 ...11 F3
Broadview CI EDN/EASTW BN20 ...11 F3
Broadwater Wy LW/ROSE BN22 ...17 H2
The Broadway LW/ROSE BN22 ...17 H1
Brocks Gyhll EDN/EASTW BN20 ...11 G4

Brodie PI EAST BN21 ......22 B1
Brodrick CI LW/ROSE BN22 ......17 H1
Brodrick Rd LW/ROSE BN22 ...12 B5
Bromley CI LGNY BN23 ......13 G5
Brookland CI PEV BN24 ......15 G1
Brookmead CI LW/ROSE BN22 ...2 E1
Brookside Av POLE BN26 ......8 B5
Brook St POLE BN26 ......11 F1
Broom CI LW/ROSE BN22 ......12 B5
Broomfield St
  EDN/EASTW BN20 ......22 A1
Brown Jack Av POLE BN26 ......11 F1
The Brow EDN/EASTW BN20 ...20 B3
Brydges CI LW/ROSE BN22 ...18 C4
Buckhurst CI EDN/EASTW BN20...16 D2
Burfield Rd LW/ROSE BN22 ......3 F5
Burleigh PI LW/ROSE BN22 ......3 F5
Burlington PI EAST BN21 ......23 E3
Burlington Rd EAST BN21 ......2 E7
Burlow CI LW/ROSE BN22 ......12 A4
Burnside POLE BN26 ......11 G1
Burrow Down
  EDN/EASTW BN20 ......16 C5
Burton Rd EAST BN21 ......17 F4
Burwash CI LGNY BN23 ......13 F3
Busheyfields HAIL BN27 ......6 C1
Buttermere Wy LGNY BN23 ......13 G3
Butts Fld HAIL BN27 ......7 E3
Butts La EDN/EASTW BN20 ......16 C1
Buxton Rd EDN/EASTW BN20 ...22 C5
Byland CI LW/ROSE BN22 ......12 C4

C

Cabot CI LGNY BN23 ......19 G4
Caburn CI POLE BN26 ......13 E3
Caburn Wy HAIL BN27 ......6 C3
Cacklebury Av EAST BN21 ......17 F4
Cacklebury CI HAIL BN27 ......6 C3
Cade St LW/ROSE BN22 ......12 B5
Cairngorm CI LGNY BN23 ......13 H4
Calverley Rd EAST BN21 ......2 B7
Calverley Wk EAST * BN21 ......2 B7
Camber Dr PEV BN24 ......15 H1
Camber Wy PEV BN24 ......15 H1
Cambridge Pde LW/ROSE * BN22 ...3 F4
Cambridge Rd LW/ROSE BN22 ...12 A5
Camden Rd EAST BN21 ......2 B7
Cameron CI HAIL BN27 ......6 C1
Canary Quay LGNY BN23 ......19 F2
Canterbury CI LW/ROSE BN22 ...12 A5
Canute CI LGNY BN23 ......19 F2
Carew Rd EAST BN21 ......22 C1
Carisbrooke CI LGNY BN23 ......13 F3
Carlisle Rd EDN/EASTW BN20 ...22 B5
Carlton Rd LW/ROSE BN22 ......3 G2
Carpenters Wy HAIL BN27 ......6 C3
Castle Bolton LGNY BN23 ......13 G3
Castle Dr PEV BN24 ......15 G1
Castle Rd PEV BN24 ......14 C1
Castlecross Rd PEV BN24 ......15 H1
Castle View Gdns PEV BN24 ...14 A1
Catsfield CI POLE BN26 ......12 D1
Cavalry Crs EDN/EASTW BN20 ...16 D5
Cavendish Av LW/ROSE BN22 ...2 E4
Cavendish Br LW/ROSE BN22 ...2 D4
Cavendish PI EAST BN21 ......2 D5
Cedar CI LW/ROSE BN22 ......12 A5
The Cedars HAIL BN27 ......4 D5
Central Av EDN/EASTW BN20 ...22 B4
  POLE BN26 ......8 D5
The Centre POLE * BN26 ......11 G1
Ceylon PI LW/ROSE BN22 ......2 E6
Chaffinch Rd LGNY BN23 ......13 G5
Chailey CI LGNY BN23 ......19 E1
Chalk Farm CI EDN/EASTW BN20...16 D1
Chalvington Rd EAST BN21 ......17 E3
Chamberlain Rd EAST BN21 ......22 A1
Channel View Rd
  LW/ROSE BN22 ......3 H1
  PEV BN24 ......15 G2
The Chantry EAST * BN21 ......22 C1
Chapel Barn CI HAIL BN27 ......7 E2
Charles Moore Ct POLE * BN26 ...8 C5
Charleston Rd EAST BN21 ......2 D2
Chatfield Crs LW/ROSE BN22 ...17 E1
Chatsworth Gdns
  EDN/EASTW BN20 ......22 D5
Chawbrook Ms LW/ROSE * BN22...2 E3
Chawbrook Rd LW/ROSE BN22 ...2 E3
Chelworth Rd LW/ROSE BN22 ...12 B5
Cherry Garden Rd
  EDN/EASTW BN20 ......21 H2
Cherry Side HAIL BN27 ......6 C2
Cherwell CI POLE BN26 ......12 D2
Chesnut CI HAIL BN27 ......4 C5

Chesterfield Gdns
  EDN/EASTW BN20 ......22 C5
Chesterfield Rd EDN/EASTW BN20 22 C5
Chestnut Dr POLE BN26 ......11 G1
Cheviot CI LGNY BN23 ......13 G4
Chichester CI LW/ROSE BN22 ...11 H5
Chilham CI LGNY BN23 ......13 H5
Chiltern CI LGNY BN23 ......13 H4
Chiswick PI EAST * BN21 ......23 E3
Church Av PEV BN24 ......14 C1
Church CI EDN/EASTW BN20 ...11 G3
Churchdale PI LW/ROSE BN22 ...18 B4
Churchdale Rd LW/ROSE BN22 ...18 B4
Churchill CI EDN/EASTW BN20 ...22 B2
Church La EAST * BN21 ......22 B2
  HAIL BN27 ......4 C1
  PEV BN24 ......14 C1
Church Rd POLE BN26 ......11 G1
Church St EDN/EASTW BN20 ...16 D1
  EDN/EASTW BN20 ......22 B2
  LW/ROSE BN22 ......12 A5
Chyngton CI LGNY BN23 ......13 E3
Cintra Vls HAIL * BN27 ......7 E3
The Circus LGNY BN23 ......18 D2
Clarence Rd LW/ROSE BN22 ......2 E2
Claxton CI EAST BN21 ......17 F5
Clayton Mill Rd PEV BN24 ......13 F2
Cleevelands LGNY BN23 ......11 H5
Clement La POLE BN26 ......11 G2
Cleveland CI LGNY BN23 ......13 G4
Clifford Av EAST BN21 ......17 E4
Cliff Rd EDN/EASTW BN20 ......25 G1
Clifton CI LW/ROSE BN22 ......17 F2
Clive Ct EAST * BN21 ......2 E7
The Cloisters LW/ROSE BN22 ...12 A5
The Close EDN/EASTW BN20 ...16 D2
  EDN/EASTW BN20 ......20 A4
Close Eight LGNY BN23 ......14 A4
Close Eighteen LGNY BN23 ......14 A5
Close Eleven LGNY BN23 ......14 A4
Close Fifteen LGNY BN23 ......14 A5
Close Five LGNY BN23 ......14 A4
Close Four LGNY BN23 ......14 A4
Close Fourteen LGNY BN23 ......14 A5
Close Nine LGNY BN23 ......14 A4
Close One LGNY BN23 ......13 H5
Close Seven LGNY BN23 ......14 A4
Close Seventeen LGNY BN23 ......14 A5
Close Six LGNY BN23 ......14 A4
Close Sixteen LGNY BN23 ......14 A5
Close Ten LGNY BN23 ......14 A4
Close Three LGNY BN23 ......14 A4
Close Twelve LGNY BN23 ......14 A4
Close Twenty LGNY BN23 ......14 A5
Close Twentyfive LGNY BN23 ...13 H5
Close Twentyfour LGNY BN23 ...14 A5
Close Two LGNY BN23 ......13 H5
Coastguard Sq LW/ROSE * BN22...3 G3
Coast Rd PEV BN24 ......15 G2
Cobald Rd LGNY BN23 ......19 G2
Cobbold Av EAST BN21 ......17 E4
Cochrane CI LGNY BN23 ......19 E3
Coldthorn La HAIL BN27 ......8 C1
College Gn EAST BN21 ......22 C1
College Rd EAST BN21 ......22 D3
Collier CI LW/ROSE BN22 ......18 B3
Collier Rd PEV BN24 ......15 F3
Collington CI EDN/EASTW BN20 ...22 C4
Collingwood CI LGNY BN23 ......19 E4
Colonnade Rd LW/ROSE BN22 ...3 F6
Coltstocks Rd EDN/EASTW BN20...22 B5
Columbus Dr LGNY BN23 ......19 F4
Colwood Crs EDN/EASTW BN20...16 D4
Combe La EDN/EASTW BN20 ...25 F1
Combe Ri EDN/EASTW BN20 ...11 G5
The Combe EDN/EASTW BN20 ...11 G5
Command Rd EDN/EASTW BN20...16 D5
Commercial Rd EAST BN21 ......2 C5
Compton Dr EDN/EASTW BN20...22 A3
Compton Place Rd
  EDN/EASTW BN20 ......22 B2
Compton St EDN/EASTW BN20 ...23 E4
Compton Ter HAIL BN27 ......7 E3
The Conifers EAST BN21 ......2 B3
Coniston Rd LGNY * BN23 ......13 G3
Connaught Rd EAST BN21 ......2 C7
Constable Rd LGNY BN23 ......18 D1
Cook Av LGNY BN23 ......19 E4
Coombe Rd EDN/EASTW BN20...22 A1
Coopers HI EDN/EASTW BN20 ...11 H5
Coopers Wy HAIL BN27 ......6 C3
Coppice Av EDN/EASTW BN20 ...11 G3
Coppice CI EDN/EASTW BN20 ...11 G3
Coral Reef CI LGNY BN23 ......19 G1
Cormorant CI LGNY BN23 ......13 G5
Cornfield Rd EAST BN21 ......2 C7
Cornfield Ter EAST BN21 ......2 C7
Cornish CI LGNY BN23 ......13 F3

Cornmill Gdns *POLE* BN26 ....11 E3
Cornwallis Cl *LGNY* BN23 ....19 F3
Cotswold Cl *LGNY* BN23 ....13 G3
Cottage La *PEV* BN24 ....9 G3
Courtland Rd *POLE* BN26 ....11 G2
Courtlands Rd *LW/ROSE* BN22 ....2 D1
Court Rd *LW/ROSE* BN22 ....12 D5
The Court *EDN/EASTW* * BN20 ....16 D1
Coventry Ct *LW/ROSE* * BN22 ....18 D4
Cranborne Av *EDN/EASTW* BN20 ....22 A5
Crawley Crs *LW/ROSE* BN22 ....12 C5
The Crescent *EDN/EASTW* BN20 ....11 G4
  EDN/EASTW BN20 ....16 D5
Cresta Cl *POLE* BN26 ....8 C5
Croft Cl *POLE* BN26 ....11 F3
Croft Ct *EAST* * BN21 ....22 C1
  LW/ROSE * BN22 ....2 E5
The Croft *EDN/EASTW* BN20 ....16 D1
Croft Works *HAIL* BN27 ....6 D2
Cromer Wy *HAIL* BN27 ....4 C4
Cross Levels Wy *EAST* BN21 ....17 G4
Cross St *POLE* BN26 ....11 G1
The Crossways *PEV* BN24 ....13 E2
Crouch Cl *EDN/EASTW* BN20 ....16 D1
Crowhurst Cl *LGNY* BN23 ....13 E3
Crown Cl *HAIL* BN27 ....6 C2
Croxden Wy *LW/ROSE* BN22 ....12 B4
The Crumbles *LGNY* * BN23 ....19 F1
Crunden Rd *EDN/EASTW* BN20 ....21 H1
Cuckmere Dr *PEV* BN24 ....13 E2
Cuckmere Wk *LW/ROSE* BN22 ....17 F1
Cuckoo Trail *HAIL* BN27 ....6 D1
  POLE BN26 ....8 C4
Culver Cl *LGNY* BN23 ....13 F3
Cunningham Dr *LGNY* BN23 ....19 E3

D

Dacre Rd *EDN/EASTW* BN20 ....22 A1
Dallaway Dr *PEV* BN24 ....13 F2
Dallington Rd *LW/ROSE* BN22 ....17 H1
Dalton Rd *EDN/EASTW* BN20 ....22 C5
Danum Cl *HAIL* BN27 ....5 D3
Darent Cl *POLE* BN26 ....12 D2
Darley Rd *EDN/EASTW* BN20 ....22 B5
Darwell Dr *POLE* BN26 ....12 D2
Dean Wood Cl *LGNY* BN23 ....13 E3
Decoy Dr *LW/ROSE* BN22 ....17 F2
Dene Cl *EDN/EASTW* BN20 ....20 B4
Dene Dr *LW/ROSE* BN22 ....17 E1
Dene Side *EDN/EASTW* BN20 ....20 B4
The Dene *EDN/EASTW* BN20 ....11 G5
Den Hl *EDN/EASTW* BN20 ....21 G1
Denton Rd *EDN/EASTW* BN20 ....22 B5
The Dentons *EDN/EASTW* BN20 ....22 A5
De Roos Rd *EAST* BN21 ....22 B1
Derwent Cl *HAIL* BN27 ....4 C5
Derwent Rd *EDN/EASTW* BN20 ....22 C5
Desmond Rd *EAST* BN22 ....3 J2
Devonshire Pl *EAST* BN21 ....2 D7
De Walden Ms
  EDN/EASTW BN20 ....22 C5
Dickens Wy *LGNY* BN23 ....14 A4
Dillingburgh Rd
  EDN/EASTW BN20 ....22 A1
Diplock Cl *POLE* BN26 ....11 F1
Diplocks Wy *HAIL* BN27 ....6 C2
Ditchling Rd *POLE* BN26 ....12 D3
Ditchling Wy *HAIL* BN27 ....6 D3
Dittons Rd *EAST* BN21 ....22 C2
  POLE BN26 ....12 A1
Douglas Cl *HAIL* BN27 ....4 D4
Dovedale Gdns *LW/ROSE* BN22 ....12 D5
Dover Rd *POLE* BN26 ....8 D5
Downlands Wy
  EDN/EASTW BN20 ....20 B5
Downs Av *EDN/EASTW* BN20 ....16 D4
Downside Cl *EDN/EASTW* BN20 ....21 H2
Downs Wy *EDN/EASTW* BN20 ....11 H5
Downsvalley Rd
  EDN/EASTW BN20 ....11 G3
Downs View Cl
  EDN/EASTW BN20 ....20 C5
Downs View La
  EDN/EASTW BN20 ....20 C5
Downsview Rd
  EDN/EASTW BN20 ....11 G4
Downsview Wy *HAIL* * BN27 ....6 D2
Drake Av *LGNY* BN23 ....19 E3
The Drive *HAIL* BN27 ....6 D3
Drockmill Cl *POLE* BN26 ....12 A1
Dudley Rd *EDN/EASTW* BN20 ....2 E3
Duke's Dr *EDN/EASTW* BN20 ....25 G1
Dunbar Dr *HAIL* BN27 ....4 C5
Durrell Cl *LGNY* BN23 ....14 B5
Dursley Rd *LW/ROSE* BN22 ....2 D4

Dutchells Wy *LW/ROSE* BN22 ....12 B3
Dymchurch Cl *POLE* BN26 ....9 E5

E

Eastbourne Av *PEV* BN24 ....15 F1
Eastbourne Rd *LGNY* BN23 ....14 B3
  LW/ROSE BN22 ....17 E1
  POLE BN26 ....11 G2
East Cl *POLE* BN26 ....11 H1
East Dean Rd
  EDN/EASTW BN20 ....20 D5
Eastern Av *POLE* BN26 ....11 H1
Ecmod Rd *LW/ROSE* BN22 ....18 C4
Edensor Rd *EDN/EASTW* BN20 ....25 F1
Edison Rd *LGNY* BN23 ....18 A1
Edmond Cl *LGNY* BN23 ....19 E2
Elderwood Cl
  LW/ROSE BN22 ....12 B5
Eldon Rd *EAST* BN21 ....17 E5
Elgar Wy *LGNY* BN23 ....14 A4
Elm Gv *LW/ROSE* BN22 ....17 H1
Elms Av *EAST* BN21 ....2 E7
Elmsdown Pl *HAIL* BN27 ....7 E2
Elms Rd *EAST* BN21 ....2 E7
Elmwood Cl *LGNY* BN23 ....13 G3
Elmwood Gdns *LGNY* BN23 ....13 G3
Elven La *EDN/EASTW* BN20 ....20 C4
Enys Rd *EAST* BN21 ....2 A5
Erica Cl *LGNY* BN23 ....13 F5
Eridge Rd *EAST* BN21 ....17 E3
Ersham Rd *HAIL* BN27 ....6 D4
Ersham Wy *HAIL* BN27 ....6 D3
Eshton Rd *LW/ROSE* BN22 ....3 G2
Eskdale Cl *LW/ROSE* BN22 ....13 F5
Etchingham Rd *LGNY* BN23 ....19 E1
Ethelred Cl *LGNY* BN23 ....19 E2
Eversfield Rd *EAST* BN21 ....2 B4
Exeat Cl *LGNY* BN23 ....19 E2
Exeter Cl *LW/ROSE* BN22 ....11 H5

F

Factory La *HAIL* BN27 ....6 B2
Fairfield Rd *EDN/EASTW* BN20 ....22 C4
Fairisle Cl *HAIL* BN27 ....4 C4
Fair Isle Cl *LGNY* * BN23 ....19 E2
Fairlight Cl *POLE* BN26 ....11 G1
Fairlight Rd *LW/ROSE* BN22 ....3 H2
Fairoak *POLE* BN26 ....12 A1
Fairway Cl *EDN/EASTW* BN20 ....22 A3
Falcon Wy *HAIL* BN27 ....4 D4
Falmer Cl *EDN/EASTW* BN20 ....16 D3
Falmouth Cl *LGNY* BN23 ....19 F2
Faraday Cl *LW/ROSE* BN22 ....17 H1
Farlaine Rd *EAST* BN21 ....17 E4
Farmlands Av *POLE* BN26 ....11 F3
Farmlands Cl *POLE* BN26 ....11 G3
Farmlands Wy *POLE* BN26 ....11 F2
Farmland Wy *HAIL* BN27 ....5 E5
Farne Cl *HAIL* BN27 ....4 C4
Fastnet Cl *LGNY* BN23 ....19 E2
Faversham Rd *LGNY* BN23 ....13 H5
Faygate Rd *LW/ROSE* BN22 ....12 C5
Fennell's Cl *EAST* BN21 ....17 C5
Fern Cl *LGNY* BN23 ....13 G4
Fern Gn *HAIL* BN27 ....4 D5
Filching Cl *POLE* BN26 ....11 E4
Filching Rd *EDN/EASTW* BN20 ....16 D5
Filder Cl *LW/ROSE* BN22 ....18 A4
Finistere Av *LGNY* BN23 ....19 E2
Finmere Cl *LW/ROSE* BN22 ....18 C4
Finmere Rd *LW/ROSE* BN22 ....18 C4
Firle Rd *LW/ROSE* BN22 ....2 E3
Fir Tree Cl *HAIL* BN27 ....5 E4
Firwood Cl *LW/ROSE* BN22 ....18 C4
Fisher Cl *LGNY* BN23 ....19 F3
Fitzgerald Cl *EDN/EASTW* BN20 ....22 D4
Fitzmaurice Av *LW/ROSE* BN22 ....3 F1
Fleming Cl *LGNY* BN23 ....14 B5
Fletcher Cl *HAIL* BN27 ....7 E2
Fletching Rd *LW/ROSE* BN22 ....13 E5
Flimwell Cl *LGNY* BN23 ....18 C4
Foley Cl *LGNY* BN23 ....19 E3
Folkington Rd *POLE* BN26 ....10 D2
Foredown Cl *EDN/EASTW* BN20 ....22 A3
Forest Vw *HAIL* BN27 ....6 C1
Fort La *LW/ROSE* BN22 ....18 D4
Fort Rd *LW/ROSE* BN22 ....18 D4
Fountains Cl *LW/ROSE* BN22 ....12 C4
Foxglove Rd *LW/ROSE* BN22 ....17 H1
Framfield Wy *EAST* BN21 ....17 F4
Fraser Av *LGNY* BN23 ....19 E3
Freeman Av *LW/ROSE* BN22 ....17 G1

Frenchgate Cl *LW/ROSE* BN22 ....12 D5
Frenchgate Rd *LW/ROSE* BN22 ....12 D5
Freshfield Cl *HAIL* BN27 ....6 C4
Freshford Cl *LGNY* BN23 ....13 H5
Freshway *LW/ROSE* BN22 ....12 A4
Friday St *LGNY* BN23 ....13 G3
Friston Av *LW/ROSE* BN22 ....17 E1
Friston Cl *EDN/EASTW* BN20 ....20 A4
Friston Downs
  EDN/EASTW BN20 ....20 B3
Frobisher Cl *LGNY* BN23 ....19 E3
Furness Cl *EAST* * BN21 ....22 D3
Furness Rd *EDN/EASTW* BN20 ....22 D3

G

The Gages *HAIL* BN27 ....7 F2
Gainsborough Crs *LGNY* BN23 ....18 D1
Gainsborough La *POLE* BN26 ....11 F1
Gallows Cl *PEV* BN24 ....14 A1
Gallows La *PEV* BN24 ....14 A1
Galveston Cl *LGNY* BN23 ....19 F3
Gardner Cl *LGNY* BN23 ....19 E3
Garfield Rd *HAIL* BN27 ....6 D2
Garnet Dr *EDN/EASTW* BN20 ....17 E3
Gaudick Cl *EDN/EASTW* BN20 ....22 C4
Gaudick Rd *EDN/EASTW* BN20 ....22 C4
Geering Rd *PEV* BN24 ....13 F2
Gemma Cl *HAIL* BN27 ....7 G2
George St *HAIL* BN27 ....6 D4
Gilbert Rd *LW/ROSE* BN22 ....3 F3
Gilbert Wy *HAIL* BN27 ....6 D4
Gilda Crs *POLE* BN26 ....11 G1
Gildredge Rd *EAST* BN21 ....2 B7
The Glade *HAIL* BN27 ....6 B3
Gladstone Cl *LW/ROSE* BN22 ....17 H1
Glebe Cl *EDN/EASTW* BN20 ....22 B2
Glen Cl *POLE* BN26 ....11 F3
Glendale Av *EAST* BN21 ....17 E4
Gleneagles Dr *HAIL* BN27 ....4 B5
Glenmore Ms *EAST* BN21 ....2 C5
Glessing Rd *PEV* BN24 ....13 F2
Gloucester Cl *LW/ROSE* BN22 ....12 A5
Glynde Av *LW/ROSE* BN22 ....17 G1
Glynleigh Dr *POLE* BN26 ....12 A1
Glynleigh Rd *PEV* BN24 ....9 G3
The Goffs *EAST* BN21 ....22 C1
Golden Miller La *POLE* BN26 ....11 E1
Golding Rd *LGNY* BN23 ....14 B5
Goldsmith Cl *LGNY* BN23 ....14 A4
Goodwin Rd *HAIL* BN27 ....4 B4
Goodwood Cl
  EDN/EASTW BN20 ....11 H5
Gordon Rd *HAIL* BN27 ....6 D2
Gore Park Av *EAST* BN21 ....22 B1
Gore Park Rd *EAST* BN21 ....22 B1
Gorringe Cl
  EDN/EASTW BN20 ....11 G4
Gorringe Dr
  EDN/EASTW BN20 ....11 G4
Gorringe Rd *EAST* BN21 ....2 B2
Gorringe Valley Rd
  EDN/EASTW BN20 ....11 G4
Gorse Cl *EDN/EASTW* BN20 ....16 D5
Gosford Wy *POLE* BN26 ....11 F1
Goudhurst Cl *LGNY* BN23 ....13 H5
Grampian Cl *LGNY* BN23 ....13 G4
Grand Pde *EAST* BN21 ....23 E4
  POLE BN26 ....11 F1
Grange Gdns
  EDN/EASTW * BN20 ....22 D3
Grange Rd *EAST* BN21 ....22 D3
Granville Rd *EDN/EASTW* BN20 ....22 D3
Grasmere Cl *LGNY* BN23 ....13 F3
Grassington Rd
  EDN/EASTW BN20 ....22 D4
Great Cliffe Rd *LGNY* BN23 ....19 E1
Greenacres Dr *HAIL* BN27 ....7 E1
Greenacres Wy *HAIL* BN27 ....7 E1
Greenfield Rd *EAST* BN21 ....22 B2
Greenfields *HAIL* BN27 ....4 C5
Green Gv *HAIL* BN27 ....6 D1
Greenleaf Gdns *POLE* BN26 ....8 C5
Green St *EDN/EASTW* BN20 ....22 A1
The Green *HAIL* * BN27 ....5 E4
Green Wk *HAIL* BN27 ....5 E5
Green Wy *EDN/EASTW* BN20 ....16 D4
Greenwich Rd *HAIL* BN27 ....7 F2
Gregory La *PEV* BN24 ....14 B2
Grenville Rd *PEV* BN24 ....15 E3
Gresham Cl *EAST* BN21 ....17 E4
Greys Rd *EDN/EASTW* BN20 ....22 B2
Grosvenor Cl *POLE* BN26 ....11 F3
Grove Hl *HAIL* BN27 ....5 E5
Grovelands Rd *HAIL* BN27 ....4 C5
Grove Rd *EAST* BN21 ....2 B7

The Grove *EDN/EASTW* BN20 ....11 G5
  EDN/EASTW BN20 ....—
  HAIL BN27 ....—
Guestling Rd *LW/ROSE* BN22 ....—

H

Hadlow Av *LGNY* BN23 ....—
Hailsham Rd *POLE* BN26 ....—
  POLE BN26 ....—
Halland Cl *LW/ROSE* BN22 ....—
Halton Rd *LW/ROSE* BN22 ....—
Hamble Rd *POLE* BN26 ....—
Hambleton Cl *LGNY* BN23 ....—
Hamelsham Ct *HAIL* BN27 ....—
Hamlands La *LW/ROSE* BN22 ....—
Hammonds Dr *LW/ROSE* BN22 ....—
Hampden Av *LW/ROSE* BN22 ....—
Hampden Park Dr
  LW/ROSE BN22 ....—
Hampden Ter *LW/ROSE* * BN22 ....—
Hamsey Cl *EDN/EASTW* BN20 ....—
Ham Shaw Ct *LW/ROSE* * BN22 ....—
Hankham Rd *PEV* BN24 ....—
Hanover Rd *LW/ROSE* BN22 ....—
Harding Av *LW/ROSE* BN22 ....—
Hardy Dr *LGNY* BN23 ....—
Harebeating Cl *HAIL* BN27 ....—
Harebeating Crs *HAIL* BN27 ....—
Harebeating Dr *HAIL* BN27 ....—
Harebeating Gdns *HAIL* BN27 ....—
Harebeating La *HAIL* BN27 ....—
Harebell Cl *LGNY* BN23 ....—
Hargreaves Rd *LW/ROSE* BN22 ....—
Harmers Hay Rd *HAIL* BN27 ....—
Harold Dr *LGNY* BN23 ....—
Harris Ct *EAST* BN21 ....—
Hartfield La *EAST* BN21 ....—
Hartfield Rd *EAST* BN21 ....—
Hartington Pl *EAST* BN21 ....—
Harwood Cl *LGNY* BN23 ....—
Hassocks Cl *LW/ROSE* BN22 ....—
Hastings Cl *POLE* BN26 ....—
Havana Ct *LGNY* BN23 ....—
Havelock Rd *LW/ROSE* BN22 ....—
Haven Cl *LW/ROSE* BN22 ....—
  PEV BN24 ....—
Hawkhurst Cl *LGNY* BN23 ....—
Hawkins Wy *HAIL* BN27 ....—
Hawksbridge Cl *LW/ROSE* BN22 ....—
Hawks Farm Cl *HAIL* BN27 ....—
Hawks Rd *HAIL* BN27 ....—
Hawkstown Cl *HAIL* BN27 ....—
Hawkstown Gdns *HAIL* BN27 ....—
Hawkstown Vw *HAIL* BN27 ....—
Hawkswood Dr *HAIL* BN27 ....—
Hawkswood Rd *HAIL* BN27 ....—
Hawthorn Rd *HAIL* BN27 ....—
The Hawthorns *HAIL* BN27 ....—
Hawthylands Crs *HAIL* BN27 ....—
Hawthylands Dr *HAIL* BN27 ....—
Hawthylands Rd *HAIL* BN27 ....—
Haystoun Cl *LW/ROSE* BN22 ....—
Haystoun Pk *LW/ROSE* BN22 ....—
Hazel Gv *EDN/EASTW* BN20 ....—
Hazelwood Av *LW/ROSE* BN22 ....—
Heather Cl *LGNY* BN23 ....—
Hempstead La *HAIL* BN27 ....—
Henfield Rd *LW/ROSE* BN23 ....—
Hengist Cl *LGNY* BN23 ....—
Hereward Rd *LGNY* BN23 ....—
Heron Cl *LGNY* BN23 ....—
Heron Rdg *POLE* BN26 ....—
Hever Cl *LGNY* BN23 ....—
Hickling Cl *LGNY* BN23 ....—
Hide Hollow *LGNY* BN23 ....—
High Cl *EDN/EASTW* BN20 ....—
High St *EAST* BN21 ....—
  HAIL BN27 ....—
  PEV BN24 ....—
  POLE BN26 ....—
High View Ct
  EDN/EASTW * BN20 ....—
Hilary Cl *POLE* BN26 ....—
Hill Rd *EDN/EASTW* BN20 ....—
Hillside *EDN/EASTW* BN20 ....—
Hoad Rd *LW/ROSE* BN22 ....—
Hobney Ri *PEV* BN24 ....—
Hockington La
  EDN/EASTW BN20 ....—
Hodcombe Cl *LGNY* BN23 ....—
Hogarth Rd *LGNY* BN23 ....—
Holbrook Cl *EDN/EASTW* BN20 ....—
Holly Cl *HAIL* BN27 ....—
Holly Pl *LW/ROSE* BN22 ....—

olt HAIL BN27 ......6 C3
ead Cl HAIL BN27 ....4 C5
rell Cl EDN/EASTW BN20 ...25 C1
well Rd EDN/EASTW BN20 ..25 G1
wood Cl LW/ROSE BN22 ...18 B4
crag Cl POLE BN26 ......8 B3
ysuckle Cl HAIL BN27 ...6 D4
................13 F4
rway Cl POLE BN26 ...11 F4
ng Cl LGNY BN23 ...19 E3
dns EDN/EASTW BN20 ...16 D1
ng Cl LGNY BN23 ...13 F3
e Rd LW/ROSE BN22 ...18 B3
tt Dr HAIL BN27 ....7 F3
rd Sq EAST BN21 ...23 E4
ett Dr HAIL BN27 ...4 D4
etts Cl LW/ROSE BN22 ...17 H1
Cl LGNY BN23 ...19 C3
ett's La LW/ROSE BN22 ...11 H4
ke Av LW/ROSE BN22 ...18 B4
La EAST BN21 ...22 B1
Rd EAST BN21 ...17 F5
Gdns EAST BN21 ...2 C7
Cl EAST BN21 ...2 B7
Tynings Cl
  /EASTW BN20 ...22 A5
ydneye LW/ROSE BN22 ...17 H1
eye St LW/ROSE BN22 ...3 G2
ion Av POLE BN26 ...11 E1
Cl POLE BN26 ...9 E5

I

t LW/ROSE BN22 ...13 E5
Mill Cl PEV BN24 ...13 F2
ms Wy HAIL BN27 ...6 C4
s Dr PEV BN24 ...15 E3
l HAIL BN27 ...4 C3
r EAST BN21 ...2 B6

J

'Dandy Cl EAST * BN21 ...17 E3
ca Wy LGNY BN23 ...19 F2
LGNY BN23 ...13 G5
e Cl LGNY BN23 ...19 F4
on Cl EDN/EASTW BN20 ...22 D5
e Cl LGNY BN23 ...14 A5
Av LGNY BN23 ...19 E4
gton Gdns
  /EASTW BN20 ...22 D4
ns La East LW/ROSE BN22 ...12 B4
ns La West
  /ROSE BN22 ...12 A4
on Rd EAST BN21 ...2 C6
on St POLE BN26 ...11 H1

K

ett Cl POLE BN26 ...12 D2
Ct EDN/EASTW * BN20 ...16 D4
ra Ter LW/ROSE BN22 ...3 F2
el Ct HAIL BN27 ...7 F2
Cl LGNY BN23 ...19 E1
West LGNY BN23 ...19 E1
'n Ter EAST * BN21 ...2 C2
St LW/ROSE BN22 ...3 F3
rick Cl LGNY BN23 ...13 H4
uns Av LW/ROSE BN22 ...18 B4
Edward's Pde
  /EASTW BN20 ...25 G1
isher Dr LGNY BN23 ...13 G5
s Av EAST BN21 ...17 G5
Cl EAST BN21 ...2 A1
T BN21 ...17 G5
s Dr EAST BN21 ...17 E2
mere Wy LGNY BN23 ...19 E2
ton Rd LW/ROSE BN22 ...12 D5
all Cl LW/ROSE BN22 ...12 C4
Wy EDN/EASTW BN20 ...16 D5
ts Gdn HAIL BN27 ...6 D3
Rd LW/ROSE BN22 ...13 E5

L

ands Cl LW/ROSE BN22 ...13 E5
am Cl EAST BN21 ...22 C1
Rd LGNY BN23 ...13 H4
ourn Av POLE BN26 ...13 E2
ng Wy POLE BN26 ...11 F3

Langdale Cl LGNY BN23 ...13 C3
Langney Gn LGNY BN23 ...19 E2
Langney Ri LGNY BN23 ...13 H5
Langney Rd EAST BN21 ...2 E6
Lansdowne Crs HAIL BN27 ...4 C4
Lansdowne Dr HAIL BN27 ...4 C4
Lansdowne Gdns HAIL BN27 ...4 C4
Lansdowne Rd HAIL BN27 ...4 C4
Lansdowne Ter EAST * BN21 ...23 E4
Lansdowne Wy HAIL BN27 ...4 C3
Lapwing Cl LGNY BN23 ...13 G5
Larch Gdns EDN/EASTW BN20 ...12 B4
Larkspur Cl LGNY BN23 ...13 F4
Lascelles Ter EAST BN21 ...23 E4
Latimer Rd LW/ROSE BN22 ...3 G5
Laughton Cl LGNY BN23 ...13 G3
Lavender Cl LGNY BN23 ...13 F4
Lawns Av EAST BN21 ...22 B1
The Lawns EDN/EASTW * BN20 ...16 D1
  HAIL * BN27 ...7 E3
  LW/ROSE * BN22 ...3 G1
Lawrence Cl LGNY BN23 ...18 D1
Leaf Gln EAST * BN21 ...22 C1
Leaf Hall Rd LW/ROSE BN22 ...3 F5
Leaf Rd EAST BN21 ...2 D5
Leeds Av LGNY BN23 ...18 D2
Leeward Quay LGNY BN23 ...19 F2
Lennox Cl EDN/EASTW BN20 ...16 D5
Lepeland HAIL BN27 ...4 C5
Letheren Pl EDN/EASTW BN20...22 B2
Levett Av POLE BN26 ...9 E5
Levett Cl POLE BN26 ...12 A1
Levett Rd POLE BN26 ...12 A1
Levett Wy POLE BN26 ...12 A1
Lewes Rd EAST BN21 ...2 B3
  POLE BN26 ...10 B1
Leyland Rd PEV BN24 ...15 F3
Lilac Cl LW/ROSE BN22 ...12 B5
The Limes EAST * BN21 ...22 C1
Limetree Av LW/ROSE BN22 ...12 B4
Lincoln Cl EDN/EASTW BN20 ...22 A5
Linden Cl LW/ROSE BN22 ...12 C4
Linden Gv HAIL BN27 ...5 E3
Lindfield Dr HAIL BN27 ...6 D2
Lindfield Rd LW/ROSE BN22 ...17 F1
Lindon Cl EDN/EASTW BN20 ...20 B4
Lindsay Cl EDN/EASTW BN20 ...22 A3
Link Rd EDN/EASTW BN20 ...20 C3
The Link EDN/EASTW BN20 ...20 C3
Linkway EDN/EASTW BN20 ...16 C3
Linnet Cl LGNY BN23 ...13 G5
Lion Hl PEV BN24 ...13 F2
Lion House Pk HAIL * BN27 ...7 G3
Lion La LW/ROSE BN22 ...3 F6
Lismore Rd EAST BN21 ...2 D7
Lister Rd LGNY BN23 ...18 A1
Lodge Av LW/ROSE BN22 ...12 A5
London Rd HAIL BN27 ...4 C4
Long Acre Cl EAST BN21 ...17 F5
Long Beach Ms LGNY BN23 ...19 H1
Long Beach Vw LGNY BN23 ...19 H1
Longland Rd EDN/EASTW BN20...22 A1
Longstone Rd EAST BN21 ...2 C6
Lordslaine Cl EDN/EASTW BN20...22 A5
Lottbridge Dro LW/ROSE BN22 ...17 H1
Lower Rd EAST BN21 ...22 B1
Lower St EDN/EASTW BN20 ...20 B5
The Lowlands HAIL BN27 ...4 C5
Lowther Cl LGNY BN23 ...13 H4
Loxwood Cl LW/ROSE BN22 ...17 G5
Lullington Cl EAST BN21 ...17 E2
Lundy Wk HAIL BN27 ...4 B4
Lushington La EAST BN21 ...2 C7
Lushington Rd EAST BN21 ...2 C7
Luton Cl EAST BN21 ...17 E4
Lydd Cl LGNY BN23 ...13 H5
Lynholm Rd POLE BN26 ...11 H1

M

Macmillan Dr EAST BN21 ...17 E5
Madeira Wy LGNY BN23 ...19 F2
Magdalen Cl LGNY BN23 ...13 G4
Magellan Wy LGNY BN23 ...19 G4
Magnolia Dr LW/ROSE BN22 ...12 B5
Magpie Rd LGNY BN23 ...13 G4
Malcolm Gdns POLE BN26 ...8 C5
Mallard Cl LW/ROSE BN22 ...17 H1
Manifold Rd LW/ROSE BN22 ...3 F5
Manor Cl EDN/EASTW BN20 ...11 G5
Manor Park Rd HAIL BN27 ...4 C4
Manor Rd EAST BN21 ...13 E5
Manor Wy EDN/EASTW BN20 ...16 D2
  POLE BN26 ...11 G1
Manvers Rd EDN/EASTW BN20 ...21 H2

Maple Ct HAIL BN27 ...6 C1
Maplehurst Rd LW/ROSE BN22 ...12 B5
Mapleleaf Gdns POLE BN26 ...8 C5
Maple Rd LGNY BN23 ...18 D3
Marcia Cl EDN/EASTW BN20 ...16 C2
Maresfield Dr PEV BN24 ...15 G1
Marina Wk LGNY BN23 ...19 E2
Marina Cl PEV BN24 ...15 H1
Marine Ct PEV * BN24 ...15 F2
Marine Gdns EAST * BN21 ...2 E7
Marine Pde LW/ROSE BN22 ...3 F7
Marine Parade Rd
  LW/ROSE BN22 ...3 F6
Marine Rd LW/ROSE BN22 ...3 F6
  PEV BN24 ...15 F2
Market Hl HAIL BN27 ...7 E2
Market St HAIL BN27 ...7 E2
Mark La EAST BN21 ...2 B5
Marlborough Cl LGNY BN23 ...13 H4
Marlow Av LW/ROSE BN22 ...2 E3
Marsden Rd LGNY BN23 ...19 E1
Marshall Rd EDN/EASTW BN20 ...18 A2
Marshfoot La HAIL BN27 ...5 F3
Martello Rd LW/ROSE BN22 ...18 D4
Martletts EAST * BN22 ...11 H4
Maryan Ct HAIL BN27 ...6 D1
Matlock Rd EDN/EASTW BN20 ...18 D5
Maxfield Cl EDN/EASTW BN20 ...16 D5
Mayfair Cl POLE BN26 ...11 F3
Mayfield Pl LW/ROSE BN22 ...2 C3
Maywood Av LW/ROSE BN22 ...12 B5
Meadow Cl HAIL BN27 ...4 D5
Meadowlands Av
  LW/ROSE BN22 ...12 B5
Meadow Rd LW/ROSE BN22 ...11 H5
Meads Brow EDN/EASTW BN20 ...22 B5
Meads Rd EDN/EASTW BN20 ...22 C4
Meads St EDN/EASTW BN20 ...22 C5
Medina Dr PEV BN24 ...13 F2
Medway HAIL BN27 ...4 C4
Medway La PEV BN24 ...13 E2
Melbourne Rd LW/ROSE BN22 ...2 E5
Melrose Cl HAIL BN27 ...6 C1
Melvill La EDN/EASTW BN20 ...16 D2
Mendip Av LGNY BN23 ...13 G4
Meon Cl EAST BN21 ...13 G4
Michel Cl EDN/EASTW BN20 ...20 B4
Michel Dene Cl
  EDN/EASTW * BN20 ...20 C4
Michel Dene Rd
  EDN/EASTW BN20 ...20 B4
Michel Gv EAST BN21 ...22 B1
Michelham Cl LGNY BN23 ...13 E3
Middleham Wy LGNY BN23 ...13 G3
Middleton Dr LGNY BN23 ...19 E3
Midhurst Rd LW/ROSE BN22 ...12 D5
Milfoil Dr LGNY BN23 ...13 F4
Milland Ms HAIL * BN27 ...4 D5
Milland Rd HAIL BN27 ...4 D5
Millbrook Gdns
  EDN/EASTW BN20 ...16 D4
Mill Cl EDN/EASTW BN20 ...20 A4
  POLE BN26 ...11 F3
Millers Ri HAIL BN27 ...6 C3
Mill Gap Rd EAST BN21 ...2 A4
Mill La HAIL BN27 ...7 E2
The Millrace POLE BN26 ...11 F3
Mill Rd EAST BN21 ...17 F5
  HAIL BN27 ...7 E3
Millstream Gdns POLE BN26 ...11 F3
Mill View Cl PEV BN24 ...13 H1
Millward Rd PEV BN24 ...15 E4
Mill Wy POLE BN26 ...11 E4
Milnthorpe Gdns
  EDN/EASTW * BN20 ...22 C5
Milnthorpe Rd
  EDN/EASTW BN20 ...22 C5
Milton Crs EAST BN21 ...22 A1
Milton Rd EAST BN21 ...22 A1
Milton St PEV BN24 ...13 E1
Mimosa Cl PEV BN24 ...8 C4
Mimram Rd PEV BN24 ...13 E2
Minster Cl POLE BN26 ...8 C5
Moat Croft Rd EAST BN21 ...22 C2
Mole Cl LGNY BN23 ...13 G2
Monarch Gdns LGNY BN23 ...19 E1
Mona Rd LW/ROSE BN22 ...3 F2
Monceux Rd EDN/EASTW BN20...22 A2
Montague Wy PEV BN24 ...14 B2
Montfort Cl PEV BN24 ...14 B1
Montfort Rd PEV BN24 ...14 B1
The Moorings
  EDN/EASTW BN20 ...22 C5
Mortain Rd PEV BN24 ...14 B1
Mortimer Gdns POLE BN26 ...11 F3
Mortimer Rd LW/ROSE BN22 ...18 A4
Motcombe La EAST BN21 ...22 B1

Motcombe Rd EAST BN21 ...22 B1
Mountain Ash Cl HAIL BN27 ...6 C1
Mountbatten Dr LGNY BN23 ...19 E3
Mountney Dr PEV BN24 ...15 H1
Mountney Rd EAST BN21 ...22 A1
Mount Rd EDN/EASTW BN20 ...22 D5
The Mount EDN/EASTW * BN20 ...22 C4
  HAIL BN27 ...7 E3
Mount View Ter HAIL BN27 ...7 E3
Moy Av LW/ROSE BN22 ...2 E2
Mulberry Cl LW/ROSE BN22 ...12 C4
Myrtle Rd LW/ROSE BN22 ...18 D4

N

Naomi Cl EDN/EASTW BN20 ...22 C4
Nelson Dr LGNY BN23 ...19 E4
Netherfield Av LGNY BN23 ...14 B5
Nevill Av LW/ROSE BN22 ...17 G1
Neville Rd LW/ROSE BN22 ...2 E3
New Barn Cl HAIL BN27 ...7 E3
Newick Rd EDN/EASTW BN20 ...17 E4
New Langney Ct LGNY * BN23 ...19 E1
New Pl EAST BN21 ...22 B2
New Rd HAIL BN27 ...5 E2
  LW/ROSE BN22 ...2 E4
  POLE BN26 ...11 H1
Newton Pk HAIL BN27 ...7 F2
New Upperton Rd EAST BN21 ...22 C1
New Vls POLE * BN26 ...11 H1
Nightingale Cl LGNY BN23 ...13 G5
Nodes La HAIL BN27 ...5 H2
Norman Rd PEV BN24 ...15 F3
North Av EDN/EASTW BN20 ...16 D5
Northbourne Rd LW/ROSE BN22...18 B3
North Cl POLE BN26 ...8 D5
Northern Av POLE BN26 ...8 D5
Northfield POLE BN26 ...11 F2
North Heath Cl HAIL * BN27 ...5 E4
Northiam Rd EDN/EASTW BN20 ...22 A1
North Rd PEV BN24 ...15 F3
North St EAST BN21 ...2 E6
  HAIL BN27 ...4 B2
  HAIL BN27 ...6 D1
Norway Rd LW/ROSE BN22 ...18 D4
Nursery Cl HAIL BN27 ...7 E1
  POLE BN26 ...11 H1
Nuthatch Rd LGNY BN23 ...13 G5
Nutley Mill Rd PEV BN24 ...13 F2

O

Oaklands PEV BN24 ...13 H1
Oaklands Cl POLE BN26 ...11 H1
Oaklands Wy HAIL BN27 ...6 C3
Oakleaf Dr POLE BN26 ...8 C5
Oak Tree La LGNY BN23 ...13 G3
Oak Tree Wy HAIL BN27 ...5 E4
Observatory Vw HAIL BN27 ...7 F2
Ocklynge Av EAST * BN21 ...22 B1
Ocklynge Rd EAST BN21 ...22 B1
Offham Cl LW/ROSE BN22 ...12 D3
Okehurst Rd EAST BN21 ...22 A2
Old Barn Cl EDN/EASTW BN20 ...16 D1
Old Camp Rd EDN/EASTW BN20 ...22 A3
Old Dr POLE BN26 ...11 F1
Old Dro LGNY BN23 ...13 G4
Oldfield Av EDN/EASTW BN20 ...11 G4
Oldfield Crs HAIL BN27 ...4 D5
Oldfield Rd EDN/EASTW BN20 ...11 G4
Old Mansion Cl EDN/EASTW BN20...16 C2
Old Mill Cl HAIL * BN27 ...6 D1
Old Mill La POLE BN26 ...11 E4
Old Motcombe Ms EAST BN21 ...22 B1
Old Orchard Pl HAIL BN27 ...6 D2
Old Orchard Rd EAST BN21 ...2 A7
Old Rd HAIL BN27 ...5 H1
Old School La POLE * BN26 ...8 C5
Old Swan La HAIL BN27 ...7 F4
Old Willingdon Rd
  EDN/EASTW BN20 ...20 A4
Old Wish Rd EAST BN21 ...22 D4
The Orchard EDN/EASTW * BN20...16 D2
Orchid Cl LGNY BN23 ...13 F4
Orion Cl HAIL BN27 ...7 F1
Osborne Rd EDN/EASTW BN20 ...21 H4
Otham Court La POLE BN26 ...8 C4
Otham Rd LW/ROSE BN22 ...13 E5
Ottenham Cl POLE BN26 ...11 H1
Oulton Cl LGNY BN23 ...13 F4
The Outlook EDN/EASTW BN20 ...20 B4
Oxendean Gdns LW/ROSE BN22 ...11 H3
Oxford Rd LW/ROSE BN22 ...3 F4

P

Pacific Dr LGNY BN23 ....14 C5
Paddock Gdns POLE BN26 ....11 F3
The Paddocks HAIL BN27 ....4 C4
The Paddock LW/ROSE BN22 ......12 D5
Pagham Cl PEV BN24 ....13 F3
Palliser Cl LGNY BN23 ....19 E4
Palma Cl POLE BN26 ....8 C5
The Parade PEV BN24 ....15 G2
Paradise Cl EDN/EASTW BN20 ....22 B3
Paradise Dr EDN/EASTW BN20 ....22 B4
The Paragon EDN/EASTW BN20 ...11 F4
Park Av EAST BN21 ....17 E3
Park Cl EDN/EASTW BN20 ....22 B2
HAIL BN27 ....6 D3
Park Cft POLE BN26 ....11 G3
Parker Cl EAST BN21 ....17 G5
Parkfield Av LW/ROSE BN22 ......17 F1
Park Ga HAIL BN27 ....5 F3
Park La EAST BN21 ....17 E2
Park Rd HAIL BN27 ....4 D3
Park Vw LGNY * BN23 ....18 C3
Parkway EDN/EASTW BN20 ......16 D2
Parry Cl LGNY BN23 ....14 A4
Parsonage Rd EAST BN21 ....22 B1
Pashley Rd EDN/EASTW BN20 ...21 H3
Patcham Mill Rd PEV BN24 ......13 F2
Paul Cl HAIL BN27 ....4 C3
Peakdean Cl EDN/EASTW BN20 ...20 B3
Peakdean La EDN/EASTW BN20 ...20 B3
Pebble Rd PEV BN24 ....15 G2
Peelings La PEV BN24 ....13 F1
Pelham Cl PEV BN24 ....14 B2
Pelham Crs HAIL BN27 ....7 E3
Pembroke Cl HAIL BN27 ....5 E3
Pembury Rd LGNY BN23 ....18 D1
Penhale Rd LW/ROSE BN22 ....3 J2
Pennine Wy LGNY BN23 ....13 H3
Penrith Wy LGNY BN23 ....13 G3
Pensford Dr LGNY BN23 ....13 H5
Pentland Cl LGNY BN23 ....13 H4
Peppercombe Rd
    EDN/EASTW BN20 ....21 H1
Percival Crs LW/ROSE BN22 ......12 D4
Percival Rd LW/ROSE BN22 ......12 D4
Petworth Pl LW/ROSE BN22 ......12 C5
Pevensey Bay Rd LGNY BN23 ....19 F2
Pevensey Park Rd PEV BN24 .....14 B1
Pevensey Rd EAST BN21 ....2 E6
POLE BN26 ....11 H1
Peyton Cl LGNY BN23 ....19 F3
Phoenix Dr LGNY BN23 ....19 G2
Piltdown Wy LW/ROSE BN22 ....13 H3
Pine Wy HAIL BN27 ....6 C2
Pinewood Cl LW/ROSE BN22 ....12 B5
Pitcairn Av LGNY BN23 ....14 D5
Pitreavie Dr HAIL BN27 ....6 C1
Plover Cl LGNY BN23 ....13 G5
Plumpton Cl LW/ROSE BN22 ....13 E3
Plymouth Cl LGNY BN23 ....19 F2
Pocock's Rd EAST BN21 ....17 F5
Polegate By-Pass POLE BN26 ....8 B5
Porters Wy POLE BN26 ....11 G1
Portland Cl HAIL BN27 ....4 C5
The Portlands LGNY BN23 ....19 F3
Port Rd LW/ROSE BN22 ....18 A1
Portsdown Wy
    EDN/EASTW BN20 ....11 H5
Pound Cl LGNY BN23 ....19 F4
Prideaux Rd EAST BN21 ....2 A2
Primrose Cl LGNY BN23 ....13 F4
Princes Rd LGNY BN23 ....19 E3
Prince William Pde LGNY BN23 ...19 E4
Priory Cl PEV BN24 ....15 F2
Priory Hts EDN/EASTW BN20 ....16 C5
Priory La LGNY BN23 ....14 A4
Priory Orch LGNY BN23 ....19 E2
Priory Rd LGNY BN23 ....14 A4
The Promenade PEV BN24 ......15 F3
Prospect Gdns EAST BN21 ......22 B1
Pulborough Av LW/ROSE BN22 ..17 C1
Purbeck Cl LGNY BN23 ....13 G4

Q

The Quadrant EAST BN21 ....22 C1
Quantock Cl LGNY BN23 ....13 H4
Quebec Cl LGNY BN23 ....19 F3
Queen's Colonnade Gdns
    LW/ROSE BN22 ....2 E6
Queen's Crs LGNY BN23 ....18 D3
Queens Gdns EAST * BN21 ......2 E6
    LW/ROSE BN22 ....3 F6

Queen's Rd LGNY BN23 ....18 D3
Quinnell Dr HAIL BN27 ....4 D4
Quintin Cl HAIL BN27 ....6 C4
The Quintins HAIL * BN27 ....7 E1

R

Raleigh Cl LGNY BN23 ....19 E3
Ramsay Wy LGNY BN23 ....19 E3
Rangemore Dr EAST BN21 ......17 F3
Ranworth Cl LGNY BN23 ....13 F3
Rapson's Rd EDN/EASTW BN20 ...11 F4
Rattle Rd PEV BN24 ....13 F2
Ratton Dr EDN/EASTW BN20 ....16 D3
Ratton Rd EAST BN21 ....22 C1
Ravens Cft EDN/EASTW BN20 ...22 D5
Rectory Cl EDN/EASTW BN20 ....22 A2
Redford Cl LGNY BN23 ....19 E1
Redoubt Rd LW/ROSE BN22 ......3 G3
Reedham Rd LGNY BN23 ....13 F3
Regency Ms EDN/EASTW BN20 ...23 E4
Regnum Cl LW/ROSE BN22 ......12 C3
The Residence LW/ROSE * BN22 ...3 F5
Reynolds Rd LGNY BN23 ....18 D1
Reynoldstown La POLE BN26 ....11 F1
Richmond Pl EAST BN21 ....2 A5
Ridge Lands Cl
    EDN/EASTW * BN20 ....22 A2
The Ridgeway
    EDN/EASTW BN20 ....20 A4
Ringmer Wy LGNY * BN23 ....13 E3
Ringwood Cl LW/ROSE BN22 ......2 E1
Ringwood Ct LW/ROSE * BN22 ...3 G2
Ringwood Rd LW/ROSE BN22 ......2 C1
Ripley Cha EAST * BN21 ....22 C2
Rise Park Gdns LGNY BN23 ......13 H5
The Rising LGNY BN23 ....14 A5
Robin Cl LGNY BN23 ....13 G5
Roborough Cl LW/ROSE BN22 ...2 D4
Rochester Cl EDN/EASTW BN20 ...22 A5
Rockall Av LGNY BN23 ....19 F2
Rockall Dr HAIL BN27 ....4 C4
Rockhurst Dr EDN/EASTW BN20 ...16 D4
Rodmill Dr EAST BN21 ....17 F5
Rodmill Rd EAST BN21 ....17 F5
Rodney Cl LGNY BN23 ....19 F3
Roffrey Av LW/ROSE BN22 ......17 F1
Roman Cft EAST BN21 ....22 C1
Romans Wy PEV BN24 ....14 A1
Romney Cl POLE BN26 ....11 H1
Romney St LW/ROSE BN22 ......3 H1
Rope Wk HAIL BN27 ....6 D1
Rosebery Av LW/ROSE BN22 ...17 G1
Rosedale Pl LW/ROSE BN22 ....12 B4
Roselands Av LW/ROSE BN22 ...18 B4
Roselands Cl LW/ROSE BN22 ....3 G1
Roselands Ct LW/ROSE * BN22 ...3 G1
Rosetti Av PEV BN24 ....15 E3
Roseveare Rd LW/ROSE BN22 ...18 B4
Rossington Cl EAST BN21 ....17 G5
Rother Av POLE BN26 ....12 D2
Rotherfield Av LW/ROSE BN22 ..13 E3
Rotunda Rd LGNY BN23 ....18 D2
Rowan Av LW/ROSE BN22 ......12 B4
Rowsley Rd EDN/EASTW BN20 ..25 F1
Royal Pde LW/ROSE BN22 ....3 G5
Royal Sovereign Vw LGNY BN23 ...19 F4
Royal Sussex Crs
    EDN/EASTW BN20 ....16 D5
Royston Cl EDN/EASTW BN20 ...20 A4
Rushlake Crs EAST BN21 ....17 F4
Ruskin Rd EDN/EASTW BN20 ....16 D1
Rusper Rd EDN/EASTW BN20 ....16 D4
Russet Cl POLE BN26 ....12 A1
Rutland Cl EAST BN21 ....17 F4
Rydal Wy LGNY BN23 ....13 F3
Rye Cl POLE BN26 ....9 E5
Ryefield Cl EAST BN21 ....17 E3
Rye St LW/ROSE BN22 ....18 C4
Rylstone Rd LW/ROSE BN22 ......3 G3

S

Sackville Rd HAIL BN27 ....7 E3
    LW/ROSE BN22 ....12 D5
Saffrons Pk EDN/EASTW BN20 ..22 C4
Saffrons Rd EAST BN21 ....2 A6
St Andrews Cl HAIL BN27 ....4 C5
St Anne's Rd EAST BN21 ....2 B5
    LW/ROSE BN22 ....11 H4
St Anthony's Av LGNY BN23 ....18 D3
St Aubyn's Rd LW/ROSE BN22 ...3 F5
St Boswells Cl HAIL BN27 ....6 B1
St Brelades EAST * BN21 ....23 F3

St Davids Cl LW/ROSE BN22 ....12 B3
St George's Rd LW/ROSE BN22 ..3 F4
St Gregory Cl EDN/EASTW BN20 ...22 C5
St James Rd LW/ROSE BN22 ......3 F4
St John's Dr PEV BN24 ....14 A1
St John's Rd EDN/EASTW BN20 ...22 C5
    POLE BN26 ....11 G1
St Leonard's Pl EDN/EASTW BN20 ...22 A2
St Leonard's Rd EAST BN21 ......2 B5
St Martins Rd LW/ROSE BN22 ...12 B4
St Marys Av HAIL BN27 ....7 E2
St Mary's Cl LW/ROSE BN22 ....11 H5
St Mary's Cottages
    EDN/EASTW * BN20 ....22 B2
St Mary's Rd EAST BN21 ....22 B1
St Mellion Cl HAIL BN27 ....6 B1
St Michaels Cl PEV BN24 ....13 E1
St Nicolas Cl PEV BN24 ....14 D1
St Pauls Cl LW/ROSE BN22 ......12 B4
St Philip's Av LW/ROSE BN22 ....2 E2
St Vincents Rd EDN/EASTW BN20 ...22 C4
St Wilfrid's Gn HAIL BN27 ....6 D1
Salehurst Rd EAST BN21 ....22 A2
Salisbury Cl LW/ROSE BN22 ....12 A5
Salisbury Rd EDN/EASTW BN20 ...22 A5
Salvador Cl LGNY BN23 ....19 F3
Samoa Wy LGNY BN23 ....14 D5
Sancroft Rd EDN/EASTW BN20 ...21 H2
The Sanctuary
    EDN/EASTW BN20 ....21 H1
Sandbanks Cl HAIL BN27 ....6 C4
Sandbanks Gdns HAIL BN27 ......6 C4
Sandbanks Gv HAIL BN27 ....6 D3
Sandbanks Rd HAIL BN27 ....6 C3
Sandbanks Wy HAIL BN27 ....6 D3
Sandown Cl LGNY BN23 ....13 F3
Sandwich St LW/ROSE BN22 ...18 C4
Santa Cruz Dr LGNY BN23 ......19 F3
Saxby Cl LGNY BN23 ....19 E1
Saxon Cl EAST BN21 ....17 E4
Saxon Gnd EAST BN21 ....22 C1
Sayerland La POLE BN26 ....8 B5
Sayerland Rd POLE BN26 ....8 B5
Scanlon Cl EDN/EASTW BN20 ...11 G4
Schofield Wy LGNY BN23 ....19 F3
School La POLE BN26 ....8 C5
Seabeach La LW/ROSE BN22 ...3 H2
Seaford Rd LW/ROSE BN22 ......3 H1
Sea Rd PEV BN24 ....15 F2
Seaside LW/ROSE BN22 ....3 F5
Seaside Rd EAST BN21 ....2 E7
Seaville Dr LGNY BN23 ....18 D3
    PEV BN24 ....15 F2
Selby Rd EAST BN21 ....17 F5
Selmeston Rd EAST BN21 ......17 E3
Selsfield Cl EAST BN21 ....17 F4
Selwyn Dr EAST BN21 ....22 C1
Selwyn Rd EAST BN21 ....22 B1
Sevenoaks Rd LGNY BN23 ......18 D1
Seven Sisters Rd LW/ROSE BN22 ...11 H4
Shalfleet Cl LGNY BN23 ....13 F4
Shanklin Cl LGNY BN23 ....13 F3
Shannon Wy LGNY BN23 ....19 F2
Sheen Rd LW/ROSE BN22 ......18 C4
Sheffield Park Wy
    LW/ROSE BN22 ....13 E3
Shepham La POLE BN26 ....9 E5
Shepherds Cl POLE BN26 ......12 D4
Sheppey Wk HAIL BN27 ....4 C3
Sheraton Cl EAST BN21 ....22 D5
Sherwood Gn HAIL BN27 ....6 D3
Shinewater La LGNY BN23 ......13 H4
Shipley Mill Pl PEV BN24 ....13 F2
Short Brow Cl LW/ROSE * BN22 ...11 H4
Shortdean Pl EAST BN21 ....22 B1
Shortlands Cl LW/ROSE BN22 ..17 E1
Sidcup Cl LGNY BN23 ....13 H5
Sidley Rd LW/ROSE BN22 ....3 H2
Silverdale Rd EDN/EASTW BN20 ...22 D4
Singleton Mill Rd PEV BN24 .....13 G2
Slindon Crs LGNY BN23 ....19 E1
Snowdon Cl LGNY BN23 ....13 H4
Solomons Cl LGNY BN23 ....14 D5
Solway HAIL BN27 ....4 C4
Somerville Cl LGNY BN23 ....19 E3
Sorrel Cl LGNY BN23 ....13 G4
Sorrel Rd LGNY BN23 ....13 G4
Southampton Cl LGNY BN23 ....19 F2
South Av EDN/EASTW BN20 ....16 C5
Southbourne Rd LW/ROSE BN22 ...18 C4
South Cliff EDN/EASTW BN20 ...22 D5
South Cliff Av EDN/EASTW BN20 ...22 D4
South Cliff Tower
    EDN/EASTW BN20 ....22 D5
South Cl HAIL BN27 ....6 D5
    PEV BN24 ....15 H1
Southdown Av
    EDN/EASTW BN20 ....11 G4

Southdown Rd
    EDN/EASTW BN20 ....
South Downs Wy
    EDN/EASTW BN20 ....
Southerden Cl HAIL BN27 ....
Southern Av POLE BN26 ....
Southern Rd LW/ROSE BN22 ...
Southfield POLE BN26 ....
Southfields Rd EAST BN21 ......
South Lynn Dr EAST BN21 ......
South Rd HAIL BN27 ....
South St EAST BN21 ....
Spencer Rd EAST BN21 ....
Spring Cl EDN/EASTW BN20 ....
Springfield Cl PEV BN24 ....
Springfield Rd LW/ROSE BN22 ..
Spring Lodge Cl LGNY BN23 ....
Spruce Cl LW/ROSE BN22 ......
Spur Rd POLE BN26 ....
Spurway Pk POLE BN26 ....
The Square PEV BN24 ....
Stables La EAST BN21 ....
Stanley Rd EAST BN21 ....
Stanmer Dr LW/ROSE BN22 ...
Stansted Rd LW/ROSE BN22 ...
Star Rd EAST BN21 ....
Station Ap LW/ROSE BN22 ......
Station Pde EAST BN21 ....
Station Rd HAIL BN27 ....
    HAIL BN27 ....
    POLE BN26 ....
Station St EAST BN21 ....
Staveley Md EDN/EASTW * BN20 ...
Staveley Rd EDN/EASTW BN20 ...
Stevenson Cl LGNY BN23 ....
The Stiles HAIL BN27 ....
Stonegate Cl LW/ROSE BN22 ...
The Stringwalk HAIL BN27 ......
Stroma Gdns HAIL BN27 ....
Stuart Av EAST BN21 ....
Sturdee Cl LGNY BN23 ....
Sumach Cl LW/ROSE BN22 ....
Summercourt HAIL BN27 ....
Summerdown Cl
    EDN/EASTW BN20 ....
Summerdown La
    EDN/EASTW BN20 ....
Summerdown Rd
    EDN/EASTW BN20 ....
Summerfields Av HAIL BN27 ...
Summerheath Rd HAIL BN27 ...
Summerlands Rd
    LW/ROSE BN22 ....
Sunningdale Cl LW/ROSE BN22 ...
Sunset Cl PEV BN24 ....
Sunstar La POLE BN26 ....
Susan's Rd EAST BN21 ....
Sussex Av HAIL BN27 ....
Sussex Cl HAIL BN27 ....
Sussex Gdns EDN/EASTW BN20 ...
Sutton Rd EAST BN21 ....
Swallow Cl LGNY BN23 ....
Swanley Cl LGNY BN23 ....
Swan Rd HAIL BN27 ....
Swinburne Av LW/ROSE BN22 ...
Sycamore Cl LW/ROSE BN22 ...
Sycamore Dr HAIL BN27 ....
Sydney Rd LW/ROSE BN22 ......

T

Taddington Rd LW/ROSE BN22 ...
Tamarack Cl LW/ROSE BN22 ...
Tamar Cl PEV BN24 ....
Tanbridge Rd LGNY BN23 ......
Tas Combe Wy
    EDN/EASTW BN20 ....
Tasmania Wy LGNY BN23 ......
Telscombe Rd LGNY BN23 ......
Tennis Cl HAIL BN27 ....
Tenterden Cl LGNY BN23 ....
Terminus Rd EAST BN21 ....
Thackeray Cl LGNY BN23 ......
The Thatchings POLE BN26 ....
Thornwood Cl LW/ROSE BN22 ...
Thurrock Cl EDN/EASTW BN20 ...
Tidebrook Gdns LGNY BN23 ...
Tideswell Rd EAST BN21 ....
Tilehurst Dr HAIL BN27 ....
Tilgate Cl EAST BN21 ....
Tillingham Wy PEV BN24 ....
Timberlaine Rd PEV BN24 ......
Timberley Rd LW/ROSE BN22 ...
Timbers Ct HAIL BN27 ....
Tintern Cl LW/ROSE BN22 ......
Tolkien Rd LGNY BN23 ....

te Gdns LGNY * BN23 ....18 D3
d Rd EAST BN21 ....22 C1
ew Rd EDN/EASTW BN20 ....11 C3
CI EAST BN21 ....17 F4
CI PEV BN24 ....15 H1
Mill PI POLE BN26 ....11 G2
iangle LW/ROSE BN22 ....11 C4
PI EAST BN21 ....2 D7
Trees EAST BN21 ....2 D7
chs CI LGNY BN23 ....13 H4
ell Rd LW/ROSE BN22...........12 D5
rr CI LGNY BN23 ....18 D1
Barn La LW/ROSE BN22...........2 B2
ham Rd EAST BN21 ....17 F3

U

CI HAIL BN27 ....4 D4
d Rd EDN/EASTW BN20...........21 H2
Av EAST BN21 ....2 C4
Carlisle Rd
  /EASTW BN20 ....22 A5
Duke's Dr
  /EASTW BN20 ....25 E1
Horsebridge Rd
  BN27 ....4 C3
King's Dr
  /EASTW BN20 ....16 D1
Ratton Dr
  /EASTW BN20 ....16 D2
St EDN/EASTW BN20 ....20 B5
ton Gdns EAST BN21...........2 B5
ton La EAST BN21 ....2 A5
ton Rd EAST BN21 ....2 A5
Wish HI
  /EASTW BN20 ....16 D2
ck Rd EDN/EASTW BN20 ....22 A2

V

nseps Rd PEV BN24 ....15 E3
uver Rd LGNY BN23 ....14 D5
CI HAIL BN27 ....7 F2
or CI LGNY BN23 ....13 F3
n CI LGNY BN23 ....19 E3
v LGNY BN23 ....19 F4
ge Dr EDN/EASTW BN20 ....22 B2

Vicarage La EDN/EASTW BN20...........22 B2
  HAIL BN27...........7 E1
Vicarage Rd EDN/EASTW BN20...........22 B2
  HAIL BN27...........7 E2
Victoria CI POLE BN26...........8 B5
Victoria Dr EDN/EASTW BN20...........16 D4
Victoria Gdns EDN/EASTW BN20 ....21 H1
Victoria Rd EDN/EASTW BN20...........16 D5
  HAIL BN27...........7 E2
  POLE BN26...........8 B5
The Village EDN/EASTW BN20 ....22 B5
Vincent CI LGNY BN23 ....19 F3
The Vineries LGNY BN23 ....13 H5
Vine Sq LW/ROSE BN22...........18 D4
The Vintry EAST * BN21...........17 E3

W

Wade CI LGNY BN23 ....19 F3
Wadhurst CI LW/ROSE BN22...........12 D5
Waldron CI LW/ROSE BN22...........17 F2
Walker CI LGNY BN23 ....19 F3
Wallis Av LGNY BN23 ....19 E3
Wallis PI LGNY BN23 ....19 E2
Wallsend Rd PEV BN24 ....14 D1
Walnut Tree Wk
  EDN/EASTW BN20 ....16 D2
Walnut Wk POLE BN26 ....11 G1
Walsingham CI LW/ROSE BN22 ....12 B4
Wannock Av EDN/EASTW BN20...........11 F4
Wannock Dr POLE BN26...........11 F2
Wannock Gdns
  EDN/EASTW BN20 ....11 F4
Wannock La EDN/EASTW BN20...........11 F4
Wannock Rd LW/ROSE BN22...........3 J2
  POLE BN26...........11 F2
Warburton CI EAST BN21...........17 E2
Warminster Rd PEV BN24...........15 F2
Warren CI EDN/EASTW BN20...........20 B4
  EDN/EASTW BN20...........22 A5
Warren HI EDN/EASTW BN20...........21 G4
Warren La EDN/EASTW BN20...........20 B4
Warrior Sq LW/ROSE BN22...........3 G4
Wartling Rd LW/ROSE BN22...........3 H1
Warwick CI HAIL BN27...........5 E3
Watermill CI POLE BN26...........11 G2
Waterworks Rd LW/ROSE BN22 ....2 D3
Watts La EAST BN21...........22 C1
Waverley Gdns PEV BN24...........15 F2
Wawmans Ms PEV * BN24...........15 F2

Wayfaring Down POLE BN26...........10 D4
Wayford CI LGNY BN23...........13 H5
Wayside EDN/EASTW BN20...........20 B5
Wealden Pk LW/ROSE BN22...........12 A5
Wealdway EDN/EASTW BN20...........16 A1
  EDN/EASTW BN20...........21 G2
  HAIL BN27...........4 A5
  POLE BN26...........10 A3
Weatherby CI EAST BN21...........17 E2
Wedderburn Rd
  EDN/EASTW BN20 ....16 D2
Welbeck CI LW/ROSE BN22...........12 B4
Wellcombe Crs
  EDN/EASTW BN20 ....25 F1
Wellesley Rd EAST BN21...........2 D5
Wellington Ct LW/ROSE * BN22...........3 G1
Wellsbourne Rd PEV BN24...........13 E2
Wells CI POLE BN26...........8 D5
Wenthill CI EDN/EASTW BN20...........20 B4
Went Hill Gdns LW/ROSE BN22...........11 H4
Went La EDN/EASTW BN20...........20 C4
Went Wy EDN/EASTW BN20...........20 B5
Wentworth CI HAIL BN27...........4 B4
Wesley PI LW/ROSE * BN22...........3 G2
West CI POLE BN26...........8 D5
Westerham Rd LGNY BN23...........18 D1
Western Av POLE BN26...........11 H1
Western Rd HAIL BN27...........6 C1
  LW/ROSE BN22...........2 C3
Westfield CI POLE BN26...........8 C5
Westfield Ct POLE BN26...........11 C1
Westfield Rd EAST BN21...........17 F4
Westham Dr PEV BN24...........15 H1
Westlords EDN/EASTW * BN20...........17 E3
Westminster CI LW/ROSE BN22...........12 B4
West St EAST BN21...........2 B7
West Street Ms EAST * BN21...........2 B7
West Ter EAST BN21...........2 B7
Wharf Rd EAST BN21...........2 B6
Wheelwright CI LW/ROSE BN22...........12 B3
Whitbread CI LGNY BN23...........13 F3
Whitley Rd LW/ROSE BN22...........2 E3
Whittle Dr LGNY BN23...........18 A1
Wildwood LGNY * BN23...........13 G3
Willard CI LW/ROSE BN22...........18 A4
Willingdon CI
  EDN/EASTW BN20 ....16 D1
Willingdon Ct
  EDN/EASTW BN20 ....11 G4
Willingdon Dro LGNY BN23...........18 B1
Willingdon Park Dr
  LW/ROSE BN22 ....12 B5

Willingdon Rd LW/ROSE BN22...........17 E1
Willingdon Wy LW/ROSE BN22...........11 H5
Willoughby Crs LW/ROSE BN22...........18 C4
Willow Av HAIL BN27...........4 D5
Willow Dr POLE BN26...........11 G2
Willowfield Rd LW/ROSE BN22...........3 F5
Willowfield Sq LW/ROSE BN22...........3 F5
Wilmington Gdns EAST BN21...........23 E4
Wilmington Sq EAST BN21...........23 E4
Wilton Av LW/ROSE BN22...........12 D4
Winchcombe Rd LW/ROSE BN22...........2 D4
Winchelsea Rd LW/ROSE BN22...........18 D4
Winchester Wy LW/ROSE BN22...........11 H5
Windermere Crs LW/ROSE BN22...........3 G1
Windmill CI EAST BN21...........17 E4
Windmill Gn PEV BN24...........13 F2
Windmill La EDN/EASTW BN20...........20 A4
Windmill PI POLE BN26...........11 G3
Windmill Rd POLE BN26...........11 G2
Windover Wy LW/ROSE BN22...........11 H4
Windsor Rd HAIL BN27...........6 D3
Windsor Wy POLE BN26...........8 C5
Windward Quay LGNY BN23...........19 F2
Winkney Rd LW/ROSE BN22...........12 D4
Winston Crs LGNY BN23...........18 D3
Wish HI EDN/EASTW BN20...........16 D1
Wish Rd EAST BN21...........2 C7
Withyham CI LW/ROSE BN22...........17 H1
Woburn CI HAIL BN27...........4 C5
Woburn Wy LW/ROSE BN22...........12 B4
Woodcroft Dr EAST BN21...........17 E3
Woodgate Rd LW/ROSE BN22...........3 F1
Woodland Av LW/ROSE BN22...........17 E2
Woodlands CI HAIL BN27...........5 E4
Woodland V POLE * BN26...........11 F2
Woodpecker Dr HAIL BN27...........6 C1
Woodpecker Rd LGNY BN23...........13 F5
Woodside Wy HAIL BN27...........6 C5
Woodward CI LGNY BN23...........19 E3
Wordsworth Dr LGNY BN23...........14 A5
Wrestwood Av LW/ROSE BN22...........17 E1
Wrotham CI LGNY BN23...........18 D1
Wroxham Rd LGNY BN23...........13 F3

Y

Yielding's CI EAST BN21...........17 F5
York Rd EAST BN21...........2 B7

Index - featured places

nts Hospital
  /EASTW BN20 ....25 G1
rstone Hospital
  L BN27 ....5 G2
ry Youth Centre
  /ROSE BN22 ....18 C4
le Shopping Centre
  ST BN21 ....2 C6
udrey Wickens
  ool of Music
  ST BN21 ....22 C2
ew Caravan &
  mping Park
  BN24...........14 D5
y Head Countryside Centre
  sitor Centre)
  V/EASTW BN20 ....24 D4
y Head Lighthouse
  N/EASTW BN20 ....24 C5
Industrial Estate
  VY BN23 ....18 D3
shop Bell CE School
  VY BN23 ....19 E1
e County Primary School
  /ROSE BN22 ....2 E4
ton Road Trading Estate
  /ROSE BN22 ....18 A2
ld Park Industrial Estate
  L BN27 ....6 C2
rfly Centre
  /ROSE BN22 ....3 J2
Market
  ....7 E2
way Secondary School
  /ROSE BN22 ....13 E4
avendish School
  ....17 F5
al Library
  ST BN21 ....2 A6

Chaucer Industrial Estate
  POLE BN26...........12 B1
The Congress Theatre
  EAST BN21...........23 E4
Courtlands Road
  Industrial Estate
  LW/ROSE BN22 ....2 D1
Crown Prosecution Service
  EAST BN21...........2 C4
Curzon Cinema
  EAST BN21...........2 D6
Devonshire Park
  EAST BN21...........22 D4
Devonshire Park Theatre
  EAST BN21...........23 E4
Dittons Park Industrial Estate
  POLE BN26...........12 C1
Downland Medical Centre
  POLE BN26...........11 G1
Downs Special School
  EDN/EASTW BN20...........21 H1
Eastbourne Bowling Club
  EAST BN21...........2 A7
The Eastbourne Clinic
  EDN/EASTW BN20...........22 D3
Eastbourne College
  EDN/EASTW BN20...........22 C4
Eastbourne County Court
  EAST BN21...........2 A5
Eastbourne Crematorium
  LGNY BN23...........13 H4
Eastbourne District
  General Hospital
  EDN/EASTW BN20...........17 G3
Eastbourne Downs Golf Club
  EDN/EASTW BN20...........21 G3
Eastbourne & Hailsham
  Magistrates Court
  EAST BN21...........2 A7

Eastbourne Health Authority
  EAST BN21...........2 C3
Eastbourne Heritage Centre
  EAST BN21...........23 E4
Eastbourne Pier
  LW/ROSE BN22...........3 F7
Eastbourne RFC
  LW/ROSE BN22...........17 F2
Eastbourne Saffrons
  Sports Club
  EAST BN21...........22 C3
Eastbourne School of English
  EAST BN21...........2 D7
Eastbourne Sovereign
  Sailing Club
  LW/ROSE BN22...........3 J3
Eastbourne Sports Park Track
  EAST BN21...........17 G3
Eastbourne United Football Club
  LW/ROSE BN22...........3 J1
Enterprise Shopping Centre
  EAST BN21...........2 B6
Filching Manor
  POLE BN26...........10 D5
Finmere Road Industrial Estate
  LW/ROSE BN22...........18 C4
Fishermen's Club
  LW/ROSE BN22...........3 J3
Fort Fun & Rocky's
  Adventure Land
  LW/ROSE BN22...........19 E5
Glennys Estate
  LW/ROSE BN22...........3 G2
Green Street Clinic
  EAST BN21...........22 A1
Grovelands Primary School
  HAIL BN27...........4 C5
Hailsham Cemetery
  HAIL BN27...........6 D4

Hailsham Community College
  HAIL BN27...........6 D1
Hampden Park Infant School
  LW/ROSE BN22...........12 C5
Hampden Park
  Secondary School
  LW/ROSE BN22...........12 C5
Hampden Park Sports Centre
  LW/ROSE BN22...........12 B5
Harvington Business Park
  HAIL BN27...........17 H2
Hawkes Farm CP School
  HAIL BN27...........4 D4
Hazel Court Primary
  Special School
  LGNY BN23...........13 F4
Hellingly Cemetery
  HAIL BN27...........4 B2
Hellingly CP School
  HAIL BN27...........4 B1
Hellingly Hospital
  HAIL BN27...........5 F1
Highfield Industrial Estate
  LW/ROSE BN22...........18 A1
Highfield Junior School
  LW/ROSE BN22...........17 H1
Horselunges Industrial Estate
  HAIL BN27...........4 D1
"How we lived then"
  Museum of Shops
  EAST BN21...........2 C7
International Lawn
  Tennis Centre
  EAST BN21...........23 E3
Lagoon Leisure Centre
  HAIL BN27...........7 E1
Langney Cemetery
  LGNY BN23...........13 H4

Langney Primary School
LGNY BN23 .... **19** E1
Langney Shopping Centre
LGNY BN23 .... **13** G4
Langney Sports Club
LGNY BN23 .... **14** B4
Lawn Tennis Club
EAST BN21 .... **23** E3
Leap Cross Small
Business Centre
HAIL BN27 .... **4** C4
Lifeboat Museum
EAST BN21 .... **23** E4
The Lindfield Special School
LW/ROSE BN22 .... **12** B5
Manor Park Medical Centre
POLE BN26 .... **11** F1
Marshlands CP School
HAIL BN27 .... **7** F1
The Mews Clinic
EAST BN21 .... **22** C1
Mobility Centre
LW/ROSE BN22 .... **2** D5
Moira House School
EDN/EASTW BN20 .... **22** B4
Motcombe Community
Infant School
EAST BN21 .... **17** E5
Mountney Bridge
Business Park
PEV BN24 .... **14** B3
North Crescent Industrial Estate
HAIL BN27 .... **6** C2
Ocklynge Cemetery
EAST BN21 .... **17** F5
Ocklynge Junior School
EAST BN21 .... **17** E4
Park College
EAST BN21 .... **17** F3
Parkland Infant School
LW/ROSE BN22 .... **17** F1
Pashley Down County
Infant School
EDN/EASTW BN20 .... **21** H1

Pavilion Cinema
HAIL BN27 .... **6** D2
Pevensey Bay Sailing Club
PEV BN24 .... **15** E5
Pevensey Castle
PEV BN24 .... **14** D1
Pevensey & Westham
CE Primary School
PEV BN24 .... **14** C1
Polegate CP School
POLE BN26 .... **8** C5
Polegate Windmill
POLE BN26 .... **11** G3
Potts Marsh Industrial Estate
PEV BN24 .... **14** B3
Quintin Medical Centre
HAIL BN27 .... **5** E3
The Quintins Shopping Centre
HAIL BN27 .... **7** E1
Ratton School
EAST BN21 .... **17** E3
Recreation Ground,
Hailsham Institute &
Hailsham Town FC
HAIL BN27 .... **6** D2
Recycling Centre
LW/ROSE BN22 .... **18** C4
The Redoubt Fortress
and Museum
LW/ROSE BN22 .... **3** H4
Roborough Day Hospital
EAST BN21 .... **2** C4
Roselands Infant School
LW/ROSE BN22 .... **3** F1
Royal Eastbourne Golf Club
EDN/EASTW BN20 .... **22** B3
Royal Hippodrome Theatre
EAST BN21 .... **2** E6
St Andrew's Infant School
LW/ROSE BN22 .... **18** D4
St Andrews School
EDN/EASTW BN20 .... **25** F1

St Bedes Preparatory School
EDN/EASTW BN20 .... **25** G1
St Giles College
EDN/EASTW BN20 .... **22** D4
St Josephs RC School
LW/ROSE BN22 .... **3** G2
St Thomas A Becket
RC Infants School
EAST BN21 .... **2** B2
St Thomas A Becket
RC Junior School
EAST BN21 .... **2** B1
Seaside Medical Centre
LW/ROSE BN22 .... **3** F4
Shinewater Primary School
LGNY BN23 .... **13** F3
Sovereign Leisure Centre
LW/ROSE BN22 .... **19** E4
Stafford County Junior School
LW/ROSE BN22 .... **18** A4
Station Road Industrial Estate
HAIL BN27 .... **7** E3
Stone Cross CP School
PEV BN24 .... **13** E2
Summerheath Hall
HAIL BN27 .... **6** D1
Sussex Downs College
(Eastbourne)
EAST BN21 .... **17** G3
Swan Barn Business Centre
HAIL BN27 .... **7** F3
Swan Business Centre
HAIL BN27 .... **7** E3
TA Centre
LW/ROSE BN22 .... **3** F4
Tollgate Junior School
LGNY BN23 .... **18** D3
Towner Art Gallery &
Local History Museum
EDN/EASTW BN20 .... **22** B2
Treasure Island Play Centre
LW/ROSE BN22 .... **3** H3

UGC Cinema
LGNY BN23 ....
University of Brighton
EAST BN21 ....
University of Brighton
EDN/EASTW BN20 ....
University of Brighton
EDN/EASTW BN20 ....
Vicarage Fields
Shopping Centre
HAIL BN27 ....
Westham Medical Centre
PEV BN24 ....
West Rise Community
Junior & Infant School
LGNY BN23 ....
West Terrace Clinic
EAST BN21 ....
The Whitehawk College
EAST BN21 ....
White House Primary School
HAIL BN27 ....
Willingdon Cemetery
EDN/EASTW BN20 ....
Willingdon Golf Club
EDN/EASTW BN20 ....
Willingdon Primary School
EDN/EASTW BN20 ....
Willingdon School
POLE BN26 ....
Willingdon Trees
Primary School
LW/ROSE BN22 ....
Winifred Lee Health Centre
LW/ROSE BN22 ....
Winter Garden
EAST BN21 ....
Wish Tower
EAST BN21 ....
Wish Tower Puppet Museum
EAST BN21 ....

Notes

Notes

AA **Street by Street** QUESTIONNAIRE

Dear Atlas User
Your comments, opinions and recommendations are very important to us.
So please help us to improve our street atlases by taking a few minutes
to complete this simple questionnaire.

You do NOT need a stamp (unless posted outside the UK). If you do not want to remove this page from your street atlas, then photocopy it or write your answers on a plain sheet of paper.

Send to: The Editor, AA Street by Street, FREEPOST SCE 4598,
Basingstoke RG21 4GY

ABOUT THE ATLAS...

Which city/town/county did you buy?

Are there any features of the atlas or mapping that you find particularly useful?

Is there anything we could have done better?

Why did you choose an AA Street by Street atlas?

Did it meet your expectations?

Exceeded ☐   **Met all** ☐   **Met most** ☐   **Fell below** ☐

Please give your reasons

ML

continued overleaf

Where did you buy it?

For what purpose? (please tick all applicable)

To use in your own local area ☐   To use on business or at work ☐

Visiting a strange place ☐   In the car ☐   On foot ☐

Other (please state)

LOCAL KNOWLEDGE...

Local knowledge is invaluable. Whilst every attempt has been made to make the information contained in this atlas as accurate as possible, should you notice any inaccuracies, please detail them below (if necessary, use a blank piece of paper) or e-mail us at *streetbystreet@theAA.com*

ABOUT YOU...

Name (Mr/Mrs/Ms)
Address

Postcode
Daytime tel no
E-mail address

Which age group are you in?

Under 25 ☐   25-34 ☐   35-44 ☐   45-54 ☐   55-64 ☐   65+ ☐

Are you an AA member?   YES ☐   NO ☐

Do you have Internet access?   YES ☐   NO ☐

Thank you for taking the time to complete this questionnaire. Please send it to us as soon as possible, and remember, you do not need a stamp (unless posted outside the UK).

ML